CARRABBA'S
ITALIAN GRILL®

Recipes from Around Our Family Table

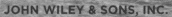

WILEY

JOHN WILEY & SONS, INC.

Published by John Wiley & Sons, Inc., Hoboken, New Jersey

Published simultaneously in Canada

For general information about our other products and services, please contact our Customer Care Department within the United States at (800) 762-2974, outside the United States at (317) 572-3993 or fax (317) 572-4002.

Wiley also publishes its books in a variety of electronic formats. Some content that appears in print may not be available in electronic books. For more information about Wiley products, visit our web site at www.wiley.com.

Co-edited by Rick Rodgers

Project Manager for Carrabba's Italian Grill: Sara Bittorf

Food Photography by Michael St. John

Italy Photography by Geoff Barish

In-restaurant Photography by Chase Strickland, Michael St. John, and Pam McClean

Family photography contributed by The Carrabba and Mandola Families

Photograph of Johhny and Damian by Jake Harsh

Library of Congress Cataloging-in-Publication Data is available upon request.

ISBN: 978-1-118-19733-2 (pbk)

Printed in the United States of America

10 9 8 7 6 5 4 3

Contents

ACKNOWLEDGEMENTS

This cookbook is a compilation of time, talent and hard work from some very special people at Carrabba's Italian Grill. Our most sincere thanks to:

Johnny and Damian, for telling your stories so we could share them with others.

Joel Barker, Vice President of Research and Development and Restaurant Operations, and Jay Smith, Senior Corporate Chef, for recipe development, book proofing, and providing the details of the lengths we go to source the best ingredients.

Ana Malmqvist, Director of Marketing Communications, and Barbara Lunseth, Print Production Manager, for art direction and producing and compiling the many photographs in this book.

Sirpa Anderson, for coordinating the countless details that enabled this book to be published.

Rick Rodgers, our writer, who so quickly picked up the essence of Carrabba's and brought it to life on these pages. Thank you for all you did to test and adapt the recipes to make them work for home cooks.

Rich Covey, Proprietor of Carrabba's East Brunswick location, for many courtesies extended to Rick and his colleague, Mary Goodbody.

Elie Massoud of Euro Mid Inc., who is a constant source of information, a valued supplier of some of our favorite ingredients, and a long-time friend of the Carrabba's Italian Grill family.

Pam Chirls, Executive Editor, Culinary, for her vision and guidance. Alison Lew of Vertigo Design, for designing a book worthy of our name. And to the many others at John Wiley and Sons, who touched this book to make a dream a reality, especially Eden Bunchuck and Abby Saul.

Carrabba's Italian Grill

INTRODUCTION

AT CARRABBA'S ITALIAN GRILL, NOTHING MAKES US FEEL BETTER THAN LOOK-
ING AROUND THE DINING ROOM AND SEEING CONTENTED GUESTS. THE DINING
ROOM IS LARGE AND AIRY, REDOLENT WITH THE AROMAS OF GARLIC, TOMATO
SAUCE, AND BASIL. IT HAS JUST THE RIGHT BALANCE OF COMFORT AND OLD
WORLD STYLE TO MAKE IT THE RIGHT RESTAURANT FOR ANY OCCASION.

On any given night, a survey of the room will show a large group celebrating a special birthday; a couple sharing a meal; a boisterous family with kids enjoying a simple supper because they were too busy to cook at home that night; and other combinations of folks that you might find at any restaurant.

At Carrabba's, we are both an extraordinary dining experience and your favorite neighborhood restaurant. This may sound like a case of dual personality, but it isn't. We want to make everyone who walks into the restaurant feel happy. This commitment to hospitality has been in place since the day we opened our doors. And it all goes back to one thing: delicious Italian food, cooked from the heart.

Almost thirty years ago, two men, a restaurateur and his nephew, both well versed in Italian cooking at both the home and professional levels, opened a small family restaurant in Texas. This book represents the amazing growth and success of those unassuming beginnings.

"My grandmothers took pride in their food," says founder Johnny Carrabba. "We learned from them and so it's the same thing here. We try to impress and to satisfy everyone who walks in the door. That is what we mean by cooking from the heart."

Johnny's uncle, founder Damian Mandola, echoes his nephew's thoughts. "Simplicity is important, as is sticking with classic ingredients and using a light hand. What brings customers back to Carrabba's is that the tomato sauce tastes like tomatoes; it's just delicious food that showcases fresh ingredients."

These words are about how a single restaurant grew into a collection of neighborhood restaurants where diners bask in warm Italian hospitality and savor fresh, authentic meals. The Carrabba's culture of excellence is based on four generations of family traditions. Our goal is to serve exceptional food in a lively, casual setting where planning and training ensures that everything runs like a beautiful, well-made clock. We hope this book is a memento of the good times you've had as our guest, and inspires you to try your hand at some of our heirloom recipes at home.

Johnny Carrabba and Damian Mandola, Founders

THE CARRABBA'S CULTURE

Carrabba's Italian Grill began as the dream of two young men who were in love with food. At first, the original Carrabba's served only the Sicilian food of Damian and Johnny's family kitchens. But as the founders traveled, the menu expanded to include specialties of Calabria, Tuscany, the Piedmont, and Lombardy. Damian says, "As long as it's Italian, we try it."

The Mandola-Carrabba family is a close-knit one with a family tree that traces its way back to Rosa Testa, who arrived in Louisiana from Sicily not knowing a word of English. Family legend says she taught herself English from the local newspaper. Arguably, Carrabba's is her legacy. There are reminders of the family's love of home-style Italian cooking across the menu:

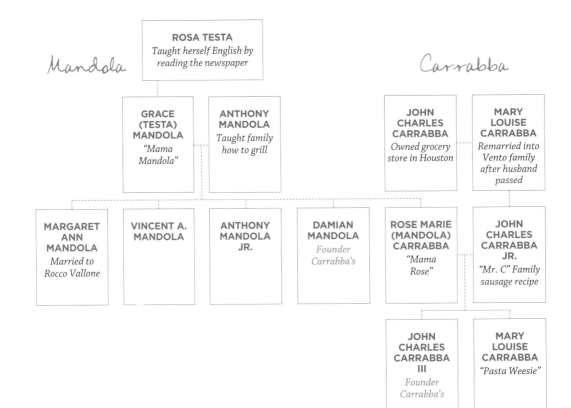

Mama Mandola's Sicilian Chicken Soup; Pasta Weesie (named for Johnny's sister Mary Louise); Pollo Rosa Maria (named for Johnny's mother); and of course, Pasta Carrabba.

Although she might not recognize them as the recipes she jotted down decades ago, many of Mama Mandola's dishes—Grace Mandola, Damian's mother and Johnny's grandmother—are still used at Carrabba's. Their integrity is never compromised.

Carrabba's operates on the essential principles of authenticity, hospitality, quality, and fun. The dishes are authentic, true to their Italian heritage and American sensibilities; the hospitality is generous and heartfelt; the food is of the highest quality, as are the surroundings and ambiance; and finally, there is an affectionate sense of fun at every Carrabba's. Our staff (we call them Carrabbamicos, a play on *amico,* Italian for friend) is ready to laugh with the customers and exhibit an easy-going attitude that makes dining there relaxing and rewarding. We promise to give you our best every time—coming close is not good enough.

But while fun is an important ingredient in the Carrabba's "recipe," so is our commitment to serious food and serious beverage. With the latter, our dedication to excellence does not stop in the kitchen, it extends to the bar. If you desire some guidance, your Carrabbamico will help you select the perfect wine for your meal. We will pour you a fine glass of wine or mix you the best martini you ever had. It's our pleasure. *Salute!*

ABOVE: *Johnny's grandparents: John Charles Carrabba and Mary Louise on their wedding day.*
RIGHT: *Damian's parents: Anthony Mandola and Grace (Testa) on their wedding day.*

IT'S ALL ABOUT THE FOOD

Carrabba's heart beats in our open kitchen. Here, you can see our respected cooks prepare your meal from scratch. It's a busy place—to say the least—and the hustle and bustle provides a liveliness that permeates throughout the entire restaurant, not unlike the warm glow from the wood-burning oven. We love the fact that the bustling kitchen shows us at work—we have nothing to hide, but plenty to show and share.

Walk into the kitchen in any Carrabba's across the country and there are some things you will *not* find. You won't find big cans of prepared pasta sauce, microwave ovens, or pre-made seasoning blends. On the other hand, you will find deep pots of freshly made tomato sauce gently bubbling on the stoves, hand-rolled meatballs waiting to be cooked, and fragrant bouquets of fresh herbs soon to be chopped and mixed. You also will see jugs of imported, fruity olive oil; fresh and dried pasta in every shape and size; large chunks of aged Romano and Parmesan cheeses; and glistening bottles of red wine and balsamic vinegars.

"When I first set up the kitchens, I insisted that everything be made on the spot," recalls Damian, looking back to the 1980s when Carrabba's was brand new. "That was how we were raised to cook and I didn't know anything else. Fresh vegetables, herbs, fish, bread. Italian food is all about freshness. Why would I buy something that I could make fresher and better on my own?" Even today, just about everything is made on the premises. The cooks prepare only enough raw ingredients to get through the next few hours, guaranteeing that the food tastes as fresh as if an Italian *nonna* had just prepared it for her family.

Soups, sauces, and braises that demand long simmering or advance preparation are started early in the day to be ready for dinner, everything else is cooked to order. In Italy, home cooks grill or roast most meats and fish, and so the cooks at Carrabba's do the same. Guests often comment on how Carrabba's food has a certain "something" that sets it apart from other restaurants. (If we were French, it would be called "*je ne sais quoi*.") We point to our wood-burning ovens and grills, and our special blends of grill baste and seasoning. (See suggestions on how to acquire that wood-grilled flavor on pages 6–7, and see the recipes for baste and seasoning on pages 145 and 146.) The phrase "Italian *Grill*" is a key to the dining experience at our restaurant.

"There's a taste profile you can't put your finger on," Damian offers. "Our approach is casual but we always have great ingredients and insist on freshness. It's not all garlic, tomato sauce, and onions. It's a lot more than that. Sure, we have tomatoes because we serve classic Italian food. Our Margherita pizza is one of our most popular and has been on the menu for a long time. It has all the elements of a classic: fresh tomatoes, olive oil, mozzarella, and basil. It's not our only pizza. We have a *rustica* pizza with eggplant, peppers and sausage, and another with red onions and salami, and then one with prosciutto and arugula."

"The Chicken Bryan is a great favorite," says Johnny. "Years ago, our family settled in Bryan, Texas, so we named the chicken for the town. It's a chicken breast with sun-dried tomatoes and goat cheese. Not exactly a down-home, Italian dish but delicious. When I was growing up I didn't eat sun-dried tomatoes and goat cheese, so with recipes such as this, we call ourselves cutting edge." In other words, we purposely have one foot firmly rooted in Sicilian food traditions, with the other equally entrenched in current culinary practices.

Carrabba's wouldn't be true to its mission without typical Italian fish and seafood dishes, such as fried calamari, mussels, and the seafood kebabs called *spiedini*. All kinds of sparkling fresh fin fish and shellfish are regularly on the menu. Of course, this is no surprise since some of the best dishes to come out of Italy include the fish and seafood of the Mediterranean, Adriatic, and Ionian seas. Notably, Carrabba's started in Houston, not far from the Gulf of Mexico and its array of seafood.

Manuel Mangiameli, Grace's brother-in-law.

Throughout this book, you will find sections entitled "The Carrabba's Way." These explain how we source the most important ingredients in our recipes, or give detailed instructions for more complicated techniques such as grilling and pizza-making. It's another way of bringing you into our kitchen, beyond just supplying the recipe.

THE RESTAURANT EXPERIENCE

Italian food is dear to America's heart. Part of this is historical because so many Americans have Italian heritage. Many of our dishes have been on our menu for years, while others are added as specials or seasonal offerings. Customers have embraced the new dishes, but they are still loyal to the ones that have been on the menu for years. You might find your personal favorite here.

Carrabba's chefs travel to Italy every year to soak up the local cooking and discover what's new and exciting at the country's best restaurants. This inevitably leads to a few new dishes on the menu back home, worthy of the customers' adoration.

Every shipment of food that comes through the back door is carefully checked before it's cooked. Great care is taken with how much is purchased, how much is prepared, and how the food is stored. We freeze as few ingredients as possible, and most of the food is held in large, walk-in refrigerators or on the pantry shelves.

Even the most common items are carefully chosen to be sure that they have extraordinary quality. We view our purveyors as our partners, and our importer has been just that to the Carrabba family for nearly 30 years. Elie Massoud, of Euro Mid Inc., met Johnny and Damian when they opened the first Carrabba's restaurant in Houston, and helped them source the authentic ingredients our recipes demand. Elie believes that every product tells a story of its own, and travels the world to hear their tales. His approach is to meet every vendor and develop long-lasting relationships with producers, which ensures Carrabba's consistent quality and supply. We often import items from Italy when the product demands it. Our antipasto olives hail from Greece and Italy, where the process of turning the bitter fruit into something delicious has been perfected. Biscotti, perfect for dunking in espresso to create the perfect light finale to a substantial Italian meal, are imported from Italy. Our balsamic vinegar is made in Modena, where it originated, and our wine vinegar is slowly fermented from some of Italy's best varieties. We season with sea salt, which has a clean, unadulterated flavor that allows the true flavor of the food to shine. But, we also have nurtured relationships with many domestic companies with Italian roots that make products in the Old World traditions.

At Carrabba's, hot food is served hot; cold food served cold. On the surface, this seems obvious, but something as basic as the temperature of a dish when it reaches the table can make or break a customer's experience. This is just the beginning. The kitchen and waitstaff at all the restaurants work in harmony to ensure that guests don't just have a good experience; they must have an outstanding experience every time.

ABOUT THIS BOOK

And now, on the following pages are Carrabba's most beloved and popular recipes based on the traditions of four generations of an Italian-American family. We have never released many of these recipes before, but instead have held their secrets close to our hearts. It's time to let our loyal customers in on some of our heirloom dishes.

Not everything in our repertoire is in this book—some things have to stay in the family—but many of our favorites are here. We understand you won't have the restaurant equipment we have, nor will you prepare the number of sauces we do in a single day. But we have carefully tested these recipes in a home kitchen very much like yours, and are confident you will happily experience our food in your home. And when you don't feel like cooking? You know where we are! We'll always be glad to see you and yours.

We encourage you to write your notes, inspirations, and traditions in the margins. The greatest compliment a cookbook can have is sauce-splattered pages.

Buon appetito!

1
APPETIZERS

"AMAZING GRACE" POMODORI BRUSCHETTE

MAKES 8 SERVINGS

amian's mom, Grace, is the inspiration behind many of our favorite dishes. Lots of restaurants serve bruschette now, but we know that details count. By the way, here's a short Italian lesson: A single slice of toast with topping is a bruschetta. The plural is bruschette.

TOPPING

1 small red onion, cut into very thin half-moons

¼ cup red wine vinegar

1 tablespoon chopped fresh oregano or ½ teaspoon dried oregano

½ cup extra-virgin olive oil

4 large ripe tomatoes, cored and thinly sliced

½ cup pitted and coarsely chopped kalamata olives

½ cup shredded ricotta salata, divided

Kosher salt and freshly ground black pepper

BRUSCHETTE

8 wide slices any crusty rustic bread

8 garlic cloves, peeled and cut in halves

Extra-virgin olive oil

8 large fresh basil leaves, coarsely torn into dime-sized pieces

1. To make the topping, soak the onion in a small bowl with cold water to cover for 30 minutes. Drain well and pat dry.

2. Whisk the vinegar and oregano in a large bowl. Gradually whisk in the olive oil. Add the tomatoes, drained onion, olives, and ¼ cup of the ricotta salata and mix. Season with salt and pepper. Let stand at room temperature for 1 to 2 hours for the flavors to blend.

3. Just before serving, preheat an outdoor grill (preferably charcoal; see page 6) or broiler on high. Toast the bread, turning once, until golden, about 3 minutes. Rub each toasted bread slice with a garlic half. (You don't have to use all of the garlic.) Place the bread on a serving platter. Drizzle olive oil over the toasts.

4. Heap equal amounts of the tomato topping, with some of its juices, over each bruschetta. Sprinkle with the remaining ¼ cup of ricotta salata and the basil leaves. Serve at once.

TIP The cold water soak reduces the strong onion flavor. Use this tip for any salad where you want the onion to play nice with the other ingredients.

CAPONATA

This eggplant relish is the hallmark of a great Sicilian cook. Johnny remembers coming home from football practice and snacking on a caponata sandwich. Now, that's Italian! Make it at least a day ahead of serving because the ingredients need some time to get to know each other. Spread it on your favorite bread and pour some wine, too.

2 tablespoons pine nuts

½ cup olive oil (no need to use extra-virgin)

1 eggplant, about 1¼ pounds, cut into ½-inch dice

1 large yellow onion, cut into ¼-inch dice

4 celery ribs, cut into ¼-inch dice

2 large, ripe beefsteak tomatoes, peeled, seeded, and coarsely chopped or 1 can (14.5 ounces) whole tomatoes, drained and coarsely chopped

⅓ cup red wine vinegar

1½ teaspoons sugar

1 cup finely chopped fresh flat-leaf parsley

¼ cup pitted and coarsely chopped kalamata olives

2 tablespoons drained nonpareil capers

2 tablespoons finely chopped fresh oregano

Kosher salt and freshly ground pepper

Crackers, bruschette, or sliced crusty bread for serving

1. Heat a large empty skillet over medium heat. Add the pine nuts and cook, stirring often, until toasted, about 2 minutes. Transfer to a plate and let cool.

2. Add the oil to the skillet and heat over medium-high heat until shimmering. In batches, if necessary, add the eggplant and fry, turning once, until golden brown and tender, 8 to 10 minutes. Using a slotted spoon, transfer the eggplant to a bowl.

3. Pour off all but 2 tablespoons of the oil and reduce the heat to medium. Add the onion and celery and cook, stirring occasionally, until softened, about 5 minutes. Return the eggplant to the skillet.

4. Stir in 1 cup water with the tomatoes, vinegar, and sugar and bring to a simmer. Reduce the heat to medium-low and cook until the tomato juice begins to thicken, about 10 minutes. Stir in the pine nuts, parsley, olives, capers, and oregano. Season with salt and pepper. Let cool completely.

5. Transfer to a bowl, cover, and refrigerate for at least 12 hours. (The caponata can be refrigerated for up to 3 days.) Serve at room temperature with the crackers.

APPETIZERS

Tip Try the calamari with the Roasted Garlic Aïoli (page 13) as a dip.

FRIED CALAMARI

MAKES 2 TO 4 SERVINGS

 f you want to check the mettle of an Italian restaurant, order the calamari. It should be crisp and tender, with just a light coating that allows the sweetness of the calamari to shine through . . . which is exactly how we make it at Carrabba's, and why it is our best-selling appetizer.

Vegetable oil for deep-frying

1 pound calamari, cleaned

½ teaspoon kosher salt

¼ teaspoon freshly ground pepper

½ cup all-purpose flour

Lemon wedges for serving

2 cups Marinara Sauce (page 141), puréed in a blender or food processor for easier dipping, warmed (optional)

1. Preheat the oven to 200°F. Line a rimmed baking sheet with paper towels. Have a second baking sheet nearby.

2. Pour enough oil to come 2 inches up the side of a large, heavy saucepan. Heat over high heat to 350°F on a deep-frying thermometer.

3. Cut the calamari bodies (sacs) crosswise into ½-inch-wide rings. Cut each cluster of tentacles in halves or thirds. Season the calamari with the salt and pepper.

4. Pour the flour into a bowl. Coat half of the calamari with flour, shaking off the excess flour. Add to the oil and cook over high heat until golden brown, about 2 minutes. Using a wire spider or slotted spoon, transfer the calamari to the paper towels to drain briefly. Move the calamari to the second baking sheet and place in the oven. Repeat with the remaining calamari and flour, reheating the oil to 350°F before frying the second batch.

5. Transfer the calamari to serving plates, add the lemon wedges, and serve with cups of the marinara sauce for dipping, if desired.

THE CARRABBA'S WAY *Grilling*

Our family has been grilling ever since Damian's father, Anthony, fired up his backyard grill, and Johnny's dad kept the tradition going. And we are sure that our Sicilian ancestors cooked many a meal over hot wood coals. At Carrabba's, we continue this delicious tradition with our menu of wood-grilled dishes but you can easily adapt our recipes to your own backyard charcoal or gas grills. And we have to admit . . . our special Grill Baste and Grill Seasoning (pages 145 and 146) also make our grilled dishes unique. We know that grilling isn't a year-round option of all of our customers, and to you we say: We are ready to grill for you whenever you wish.

- How the food is positioned over the heat source affects its cooking. Learn the difference between direct and indirect cooking.

DIRECT COOKING is cooking directly over hot coals (or the burners of a gas grill). For a charcoal grill, always have an empty area where you can move food that is cooking too quickly or dripping fat and causing flare-ups. Leave a perimeter around the mound of coals for this purpose. If flare-ups occur with a gas grill, move the food to a turned-off burner.

INDIRECT COOKING refers to food that is placed away from the heat source so it cooks by radiated heat. For a charcoal grill, heap the coals on one side of the grill, leaving the other side empty. For a gas grill, preheat the grill on high, then turn one burner off, creating a cool area. For either grill, place a disposable aluminum foil pan on the empty/cool area of the heat source. Pour 2 cups of water into the pan. Cook the food on the grate over the pan.

- Not all food is grilled over high heat! At Carrabba's, we have zones of heat on our wood grills—some are hot for searing steaks, but others are cooler for more gentle cooking of chicken and seafood. A hot grill will register 450° to 600°F, and a medium grill around 400°F.

- For a charcoal grill, use the hand test carefully. Place your hand about 2 inches above the cooking grate. If you can only hold your hand in place for 1 to 2 seconds before it is uncomfortably warm, the grill is hot. When the grill is medium-hot, you will be able to hold your hand in position for about 3 seconds.

- For a gas grill, always preheat the grill with the lid closed on High heat. Adjust the heat as needed, using the thermostat controls and lid thermometer as indicators.

- Always cook with the grill lid closed as much as possible. Fire needs oxygen to stay alive, so a closed lid reduces the chances of flare-ups, most of which are caused by the fat dripping from the food or marinade onto the heat sources. If you have a charcoal grill, the vents on the lid and underneath the kettle can be opened or shut to control the air flow. For high heat, keep the vents wide open to feed the flame. For medium heat, close them halfway to reduce the oxygen so the fire burns at a lower temperature.

- We use mostly oak and pecan logs for our fuel sources. Their deliciously sweet and smoky flavor is just one reason why our food is so tasty. The average commercial grill is not made to burn hardwood, but you can easily use oak and pecan wood chips, soaked and drained, then added to the heat source to give off smoldering, flavorful smoke. Wood chips are sold at hardware stores and online. (Wood chunks are best for long-cooked food, such as barbecue, and the wood chips take less time to soak, too.)

- We are partial to the oak/pecan combination, but the idea is to use one "strong" wood (such as oak or hickory) tempered with a "mellow" one (pecan or fruit wood such as cherry, apple, or peach). Do not use homemade chips from resinous or soft woods. To allow the most flexibility with your home cooking, we have not included wood chips in the grilling recipes, but we do encourage you to try them. Here's how:

  Soak 1 handful (about ½ cup) each oak and pecan wood chips in water to cover for at least 30 minutes and up to 2 hours. Drain just before using. For a charcoal grill, scatter the wood chips over the hot coals, and then add the food. For a gas grill, add the chips to a smoker box according to the manufacturer's instructions.

- Soak wooden skewers for spiedini well before use. They should be soaked in water to cover for at least 30 minutes and up to 2 hours, then drained. Because we use medium, and not high heat, for grilling spiedini, the skewers shouldn't scorch. However, if you still have trouble with burned wooden skewers, use metal skewers. These are inexpensive and a great investment. Skewers with flat blades hold the food more securely than round or rectangular ones.

CHICKEN SPIEDINI

*W*e love how the close proximity of the ingredients on a skewer allows them to share their flavors. This chicken spiedini may share a name with the seafood version on page 66, but they are quite different. The chicken should not be cut too large, as it must cook through by the time the bread is toasted.

HERB MIX

1 tablespoon finely chopped fresh parsley

1 tablespoon finely chopped fresh oregano

1½ teaspoons finely chopped fresh rosemary

1½ teaspoons finely chopped fresh thyme

½ cup balsamic vinegar

2 boneless and skinless chicken breast halves, about 6 ounces each, cut into 12 chunks about 1 inch square

1 teaspoon Grill Seasoning (page 146)

18 grape tomatoes, cut in halves lengthwise

12 cubes (1 inch) crusty rustic Italian bread

8 long wooden skewers, soaked in cold water for at least 30 minutes, drained

2 tablespoons extra-virgin olive oil

3 cups baby arugula

3 tablespoons Balsamic Vinaigrette (page 20)

¼ cup shredded ricotta salata (use the large holes on a box shredder)

1. Prepare an outdoor grill for direct cooking with medium heat (see page 6).

2. To make the herb mix, combine all of the ingredients in a small bowl.

3. Bring the vinegar to a boil in a small saucepan over high heat. Boil until reduced to 2 tablespoons, about 5 minutes. Transfer the reduction to a bowl and let cool. If the vinegar solidifies, stir in a little water to thin it slightly.

4. Season the chicken with the grill seasoning. On each skewer, spear 2 bread cubes, 2 chicken pieces, and 3 tomatoes, alternating the pieces so the bread and chicken are next to each other. Brush the food on the skewers with the oil and sprinkle with the herb mix. Let stand at room temperature while the grill heats.

5. Brush the cooking grate clean. Lightly oil the grate. Put the skewers on the grill. Cook, with the lid closed as much as possible, turning occasionally, until the chicken feels firm when pressed with a finger and the bread is toasted, about 6 minutes. Remove from the grill.

6. Toss the arugula with the vinaigrette in a large bowl. Spread on a platter. Top with the skewers. Drizzle the balsamic reduction over the skewers and sprinkle with the ricotta salata. Serve immediately.

TUSCAN CAULIFLOWER TOASTS

MAKES 6 SERVINGS

n Tuscany, sliced and grilled bread slices rubbed with garlic and "greased" with olive oil are called fettunte. *The recipe sounds a little like bruschette, doesn't it? Well, sometimes* fettunte *are served plain, like garlic toast, but bruschette are always topped. You won't care about the semantics when you dig into this dish, which is an appetizer on its way to becoming a salad.*

ROASTED CAULIFLOWER

1 head cauliflower, broken into florets, then cut into ½-inch thick slices

3 tablespoons extra-virgin olive oil, plus more for the baking sheet

3 garlic cloves, coarsely chopped

Kosher salt and freshly ground black pepper

6 wide slices crusty rustic bread

6 garlic cloves, peeled and cut in halves

Extra-virgin olive oil

2 cups baby arugula

2 tablespoons fresh lemon juice

1 wedge Parmesan cheese, about 6 ounces, for shaving cheese curls

1. To make the roasted cauliflower, preheat the oven to 400°F. Lightly oil a large rimmed baking sheet.

2. Toss the cauliflower, oil, and garlic together in a large bowl. Spread on the baking sheet and season with salt and pepper. Bake, stirring occasionally, until the cauliflower is lightly browned and tender, about 40 minutes.

3. Just before serving, preheat an outdoor grill (preferably charcoal) or broiler on high. Toast the bread, turning once, until golden, about 3 minutes. Rub each toasted bread slice with a garlic half. (You don't have to use all of the garlic.) Place the bread on a serving platter. Drizzle olive oil over the toasts.

4. Toss the arugula with 2 tablespoons olive oil and the lemon juice. Season with salt and pepper. Top each bread slice with equal amounts of the arugula, followed by the cauliflower. Using a swivel vegetable peeler, shave as many curls of Parmesan over the *fettunte* as you like. Serve hot.

HERB-OLIVE OIL DIP

 hen the bread comes to your table at Carrabba's, you are also served a dish of this herb-scented olive oil to dip the slices. It's a delicious ritual that many people would like to re-create at home, and now they can.

1½ teaspoons finely chopped fresh flat-leaf parsley

¾ teaspoon finely chopped fresh basil

¾ teaspoon finely chopped fresh rosemary

¼ teaspoon dried oregano

¼ teaspoon granulated garlic

⅛ teaspoon crushed hot red pepper flakes

½ teaspoon kosher salt

¼ teaspoon freshly ground black pepper

⅓ cup extra-virgin olive oil

Sliced crusty rustic bread for dipping

1. Mix the parsley, basil, rosemary, oregano, granulated garlic, hot red pepper, salt, and pepper together in a small serving bowl. Add the olive oil and stir. Serve with the bread for dipping.

TIP At Carrabba's, we sprinkle 1 teaspoon of the herb mix in a saucer, and add about 3 tablespoons of oil. At home, a single batch is more practical.

POLENTA FRIES WITH MARINARA SAUCE

If you think that French fries are irresistible, just try this baked polenta version. Let the cooked polenta chill and firm for a few hours, and then cut the solidified mass into sticks for baking. Use your imagination for other dips (maybe mayonnaise mixed with pesto?).

Kosher salt

1½ cups yellow polenta

½ cup freshly grated Romano cheese

Extra-virgin olive oil for brushing

Freshly ground black pepper

2 cups Marinara Sauce (page 141), puréed in a blender or food processor for easier dipping, warmed

1. Bring 5 cups of water and ¾ teaspoon of salt to a boil in a heavy-bottomed medium saucepan over high heat. Whisk in the polenta and bring to a simmer. Reduce the heat to low and let cook (it will make bubbles, but not boil or simmer), whisking often to avoid sticking, until the polenta is tender and very thick (it should be stiff enough to support a standing whisk for a few seconds before it falls), about 15 minutes. Remove from the heat and stir in the Romano cheese.

2. Lightly oil a 13-by-9-inch baking dish. Using an oiled heatproof spatula, spread the polenta in a smooth, thick layer in the dish. Let cool. Cover with plastic wrap and refrigerate until chilled and firm, about 2 hours, or up to one day.

3. Preheat the oven to 450°F. Lightly oil a rimmed baking sheet.

4. Invert the baking dish and unmold the polenta onto a cutting board. Using an oiled knife, cut the polenta into thirds lengthwise, and then into "fries" about ½-inch wide. Transfer to the baking sheet and brush lightly with oil. Bake until underside is golden brown, about 20 minutes. Using a metal spatula, flip the fries and continue baking until crisp and golden brown, 10 to 15 minutes more.

5. Season with salt and pepper. Heap on a platter and serve hot, with bowls of the marinara sauce for dipping.

TIP Use coarsely ground polenta, and not cornmeal or instant polenta, as it chills into a sturdier slab that is better for cutting and baking.

FRIED ZUCCHINI WITH ROASTED GARLIC AÏOLI

MAKES 4 SERVINGS

ur guests are always amazed when we tell them the recipe for our fried zucchini—dip the sticks in milk, coat with flour, and fry away. The milk helps the flour cling, but doesn't make the batter gloppy like so many recipes that have eggs in them. We've said it before and we'll say it again . . . sometimes easy is good! The roasted garlic aïoli ups the ante a bit, but they are just as delicious with a squeeze of lemon.

ROASTED GARLIC AÏOLI

1 head Roasted Garlic (see page 111)

1 cup mayonnaise

2 tablespoons fresh lemon juice

1 tablespoon balsamic vinegar

Kosher salt and freshly ground black pepper

2 zucchini, trimmed, cut into 3-by-½-inch sticks

½ cup milk

1 cup all-purpose flour

½ teaspoon kosher salt

¼ teaspoon freshly ground black pepper

1. To make the aïoli, squeeze the roasted garlic cloves out of the hull into a small bowl. Mash the garlic cloves with a fork. Add the mayonnaise, lemon juice, and vinegar and whisk until combined. Season with salt and pepper. (The aïoli can be prepared up to 2 days ahead, covered and refrigerated.) Transfer the aïoli to 4 individual ramekins or custard cups.

2. Preheat the oven to 200°F. Line a rimmed baking sheet with paper towels. Have a second baking sheet ready.

3. Pour enough oil to come 2 inches up the side of a large, heavy saucepan. Heat over high heat to 350°F on a deep-frying thermometer.

4. Mix the flour, salt, and pepper together in a medium bowl. Pour the milk into a second bowl. In batches, dip the zucchini in milk, shake off the excess milk, then coat with flour. Shake off the excess flour and add to the oil. Cook over high heat until golden brown, about 2 minutes. Using a wire spider or slotted spoon, transfer the zucchini to the paper towels to drain briefly. Move the zucchini to the second baking sheet and place in the oven. Let the oil return to 350°F between batches.

5. Heap the zucchini on a platter and serve hot, with the aïoli for dipping.

2

SOUPS AND SALADS

For centuries, olive oil has reigned as the king of oils. Throughout the Mediterranean, from Turkey to Spain, Sicily to North Africa, the olive tree has played an important role in the day-to-day life of the people. Its leaves shade the hot land, its wood is transformed into utilitarian bowls and furniture, and oil is extracted from the fruit for cooking. The health benefits of olive oil have been well documented. Rich in monounsaturated fat, olive oil can reduce blood cholesterol levels, which can decrease the chance of heart disease. And, unlike the typical vegetable oil, it has a distinct and delicious flavor that enhances the food cooked in it.

The oil from olives can be extracted by a number of methods. The simplest, and traditional, methods are by crushing or pressing. These days, mechanical methods come into play. The best olive oil is produced by the cold-press method, where no heat is applied during extraction, to yield extra-virgin oil with the most olive flavor. Heat can be applied to release more oil, which results in an oil with diluted flavor. Also, the oil can be refined or blended, again getting further away from the desirable olive characteristics.

The best olive oil should combine three basic flavors: fruity, grassy, and spicy. The first means that you should detect a full, ripe hint of sweetness in the oil, keeping in mind that the olive is a fruit, after all. A grassy flavor should be vegetal in a positive way, not like eating the front lawn. And you should be able to taste a little peppery heat. Don't worry about color too much. A deep-green color does not automatically indicate top-quality oil. And the oil's body should feel heftier on the palate than highly refined vegetable oil. All this can be determined by a taste test. If the oil has too much of one characteristic that overshadows the others, keep looking.

Because so many Italians (and Sicilians) immigrated to America, their home-grown olive oil has long set the standard for olive oil in our country. But excellent olive oil comes from other countries, too. We use a Spanish olive oil that is hard to beat. Spain is actually the leader in world olive oil production, and makes about twice as much oil as Italy, which ranks second. At home, apply the taste test to find a well-balanced, reasonably priced extra-virgin oil that you can use both for cooking and making salads. (Artisan olive oil, produced in small batches from olives in a very localized area, can be fantastic, but it should be reserved for salads or as a seasoning to pour over grilled meats. It is much too expensive to cook with.) Our oil is made just for us by the respected Spanish olive oil producer La Rambla with a blend of Arbequina, Cornicabra, and Picual olives, and not "cut" with vegetable oil, so you always get the full benefit of flavor.

Always store olive oil in a cool, dark place (but not the refrigerator, where it will solidify). It should be kept in a metal can or a dark-colored bottle to protect against oxidation from sun rays. Only buy as much olive oil as you will use within six-month period, as the oil has no preservatives.

INSALATA MISTA

 hen Johnny and Damian were kids, the family salads were uncomplicated, but always full of flavor. This mixed salad includes all of the usual suspects, dressed with a tangy, not-too-garlicky vinaigrette that may become your house dressing. Do you like other things (beets, garbanzo beans, or carrots) in your salad? Be our guest to change the formula.

VINAIGRETTE

3 tablespoons red wine vinegar

1 teaspoon minced fresh basil

1 small garlic clove, minced

1 pinch of dried oregano

½ cup plus 1 tablespoon extra-virgin olive oil

Kosher salt and freshly ground black pepper

SALAD

6 ounces (8 cups) mixed salad greens, washed and spun dry

1 celery heart (about 6 ribs), cut crosswise into ¼-inch-thick slices

1 ripe tomato, seeded and cut into ½-inch dice

1 small cucumber, peeled, cut in half lengthwise, seeded, and cut into ⅛-inch thick half-moons

1 small fennel bulb, cut in half vertically, core discarded, bulb cut crosswise into ⅛-inch thick half-moons

½ small red onion, cut into thin half-moons, soaked, if desired (see Tip, page 2)

½ cup pitted and coarsely chopped kalamata olives

¼ cup (1 ounce) freshly grated Parmesan cheese (optional)

1. To make the vinaigrette, whisk the vinegar, basil, garlic, and oregano together in a medium bowl. Gradually whisk in the oil. Season with salt and pepper.

2. Toss the greens, celery, tomato, cucumber, fennel, onion, and olives together in a large bowl. Add the vinaigrette and toss again. Sprinkle with the Parmesan, if using. Serve immediately.

TIP Dip a piece of lettuce into vinaigrette to taste and judge the seasoning— by itself, the vinaigrette will seem too sour.

SOUPS AND SALADS

PANZANELLA

anzanella is a Tuscan salad with a main ingredient of stale bread. Bread salad? Yes, but there are plenty of vegetables in the bowl, too. And the bread is soaked in water to soften it. (Modern recipes may use croutons, but this is the original recipe.) A stale loaf of sturdy artisan bread is a must for this salad to be successful . . . and maybe a sense of the famous Tuscan tendency not to let anything go to waste.

1 loaf of crusty rustic bread, about 1 pound, anywhere from 1 to 3 days old

1 small red onion, cut into thin half-moons

2 ripe medium tomatoes, seeded and cut into ½-inch dice

1 cucumber, peeled, seeded, and cut into ½-inch dice

3 cups baby arugula

2 tablespoons red wine vinegar

½ cup extra-virgin olive oil

Kosher salt and freshly ground black pepper

1. Put the bread in a large bowl and add enough cold water to cover. Top with a plate to keep the bread submerged, and let stand until the bread softens, 20 to 30 minutes.

2. Put the onion in a small bowl and add cold water to cover. Let stand for 20 to 30 minutes. Drain and pat dry with paper towels.

3. Drain the bread. Break up and squeeze the soaked bread to remove excess water, just like wringing a sponge. Shred the bread into bite-sized pieces. Transfer to a bowl and add the tomato, cucumber, soaked red onion, and arugula. Mix well.

4. Pour the vinegar into a small bowl. Gradually whisk in the oil. Pour over the bread mixture and toss. Season with salt and pepper and toss again. Serve at once.

TIP Our wine vinegar, made by Emiliani, is imported from Italy, where it is produced from fine Barbera, Docetto, and Croatina grapes and slowly aged for great flavor. Use "real," slowly aged wine vinegar, and you will taste the difference in your cooking.

CHOPPED SALAD

reen salad is a fine way to start a meal, but sometimes you need a salad that's more substantial. With everything in it but the kitchen sink (and we mean that in a nice way), this salad will fill you up without weighing you down. Feel free to add whatever is in the fridge that strikes your fancy . . . artichoke hearts would be good.

BALSAMIC VINAIGRETTE

¼ cup balsamic vinegar

1 teaspoon sugar

1 teaspoon Dijon mustard

2 garlic cloves, minced

½ teaspoon kosher salt

½ teaspoon freshly ground black pepper

¾ cup extra-virgin olive oil

CHOPPED SALAD

6 ounces mixed greens, rinsed and dried

1 romaine heart, coarsely chopped

6 ounces sliced dry or Genoa salami, cut into ¼-inch wide strips

4 ounces (¼-inch) diced fontina cheese (1 cup)

⅓ cup (¼-inch) diced carrots

⅓ cup (¼-inch) diced celery

⅓ cup (¼-inch) diced red onion

⅓ cup (¼-inch) diced fennel

⅓ cup drained and coarsely chopped peperoncini (Italian pickled hot peppers)

⅓ cup coarsely chopped pitted kalamata olives

¼ cup drained and rinsed canned garbanzo beans (chickpeas)

1. To make the vinaigrette, whisk the vinegar, sugar, mustard, garlic, salt, and pepper in a medium bowl. Gradually whisk in the oil. Makes about 1 cup. (The vinaigrette can be made up to 1 week ahead, stored in a jar in the refrigerator. Shake well before using.)

2. Mix all of the salad ingredients in a large serving bowl. Add the vinaigrette and toss well. Serve immediately.

Make a double batch of the dressing, use 1 cup to dress this salad, and
refrigerate the leftover vinaigrette for another meal.

TIP Do not add uncooked pasta to soup, or it will soak up too much broth during cooking, and make the soup very thick.

MAMA MANDOLA'S SICILIAN CHICKEN SOUP

hicken soup has legendary restorative powers, and this is the soup to eat when you aren't feeling your best. Instead of the egg noodles that an American mom might use, Grace always added little pasta tubes or broken long pasta to her soup. She also used a tough old stewing hen, but a large chicken is a good stand-in.

1 whole chicken, about 4½ pounds, giblets removed

1 large yellow onion, finely chopped

3 celery ribs, cut into ¼-inch dice

3 carrots, cut into ¼-inch dice

3 green bell peppers, cored and cut into ¼-inch dice

3 medium baking potatoes, such russet or Burbank, peeled and cut into ½-inch dice

1 can (14.5 ounces) diced tomatoes in juice

½ cup chopped fresh flat-leaf parsley

4 garlic cloves, chopped

Kosher salt and freshly ground black pepper

1 cup ditalini or other "soup pasta"

1. Put the whole chicken, onion, celery, carrots, bell peppers, potatoes, tomatoes and their juices in a large soup pot and add enough cold water to cover by 1 inch. Bring to a boil over high heat, skimming off the foam that rises to the surface. Add the parsley, garlic, and 1 tablespoon salt and 1 teaspoon pepper.

2. Reduce the heat to medium-low. Partially cover the pot and simmer until the chicken is falling off the bones, about 2 hours. Using tongs, transfer the chicken to a large bowl and let cool for about 20 minutes. Keep the soup in the pot simmering.

3. Remove the meat from the chicken, discarding the skin and bones, taking care not to mangle the meat and keeping it in neat pieces. Tear or pull the boned chicken into large bite-sized pieces. (We prefer hand-pulled chicken to chopped chunks.)

4. Meanwhile, bring a medium saucepan of water to a boil over high heat. Add salt to taste. Add the ditalini and cook according to the package directions until tender. Drain well.

5. Using a large slotted spoon or a potato masher, mash some of the potatoes in the pot to lightly thicken the broth. Add the chicken and pasta to the pot. Season with salt and pepper. Serve hot.

PEAR, GORGONZOLA, AND HAZELNUT SALAD

MAKES 6 TO 8 SERVINGS

It took time for some folks to get used to pears in their green salad. Now this combination of sweet fruit, bitter greens, pungent cheese, and crunchy nuts is appreciated for its creative blend of flavors and textures. Be sure to let the pears get nice and ripe. Domestic Gorgonzola cheese is perfect, but if you use the Italian version, "mountain" Gorgonzola is easier to crumble than the creamy "dolce" cheese.

3 tablespoons red wine vinegar

Kosher salt and freshly ground black pepper

½ cup hazelnut oil

1 head radicchio, about 7 ounces, cored and torn into bite-sized pieces

1 head frisée, about 6 ounces, torn into bite-sized pieces

1 Belgian endive, cut crosswise into ½-inch pieces, core removed

2 ripe Anjou or Bartlett pears, unpeeled, cored and cut into ¼-inch wedges

1 cup (4 ounces) crumbled Gorgonzola cheese

⅔ cup (about 3 ounces) hazelnuts, toasted, skinned, and coarsely chopped

1. Whisk the vinegar, ½ teaspoon salt, and ¼ teaspoon pepper in a large salad bowl. Gradually whisk in the oil. Add the radicchio, frisée, and endive and toss. Add the pears and Gorgonzola and toss gently. Sprinkle with the hazelnuts. Season with salt and pepper. Serve on salad plates.

TIP For homemade hazelnut oil, blend ¼ cup toasted and chopped hazelnuts with ½ cup vegetable oil until the nuts are minced, let stand 5 minutes, and strain.

Prosciutto & Pancetta

Before refrigeration, people had to find another way than cold temperatures to preserve meat. Curing, pickling, drying, and smoking are a few ways to extend edibility beyond a few days. This necessity led to the creation of two of the tastiest and highly utilized ingredients in the Italian kitchen, prosciutto and pancetta.

PROSCIUTTO To make this prime example of Italian culinary ingenuity, pork leg is cured with salt (a procedure that discourages the growth of bacteria and draws out excess moisture) and then hung to dry naturally in cool air. This unhurried procedure yields firm, flavorful meat that is usually sliced paper-thin. While imported Italian prosciutto is available, we buy ours from a domestic source in Pennsylvania that ages the pork in the local clean mountain air.

Paper-thin prosciutto (pro-SHOOT-oh) is suitable for appetizers—serve it with fresh ripe melon, figs, or pears for one of the most glorious (and easiest) of all Italian first courses. And we love it as a fresh topping for Prosciutto and Arugula Pizza (page 102). However, cooked prosciutto has its place, too, and adds its salty, slightly tangy flavor to soups and sauces. We even use it to wrap boneless pork tenderloin, creating a protective sheath for grilling.

When purchasing prosciutto for cooking, ask the counter person not to slice the meat paper-thin, as they are surely used to doing. It should be cut about ⅛-inch thick. (Packaged pre-sliced prosciutto is too thin.) At home, cut the sliced prosciutto into ¼-inch pieces. It is now ready to be cooked in a little oil to add a salty, tangy flavor to soups and sauces. Never trim the delicious, creamy white fat from prosciutto, or you will be cutting away much of its flavor.

PANCETTA Although pancetta (pan-CHET-ta) is prepared from the same cut of meat as bacon (pork belly), the similarity stops there. Bacon is smoked, but pancetta is not. And bacon is usually flat, while pancetta is rolled into a salami shape. Like prosciutto, pancetta is used in as a cooking ingredient to flavor minestrone and other soups, as well as Amatriciana and other sauces.

If pancetta is in the delicatessen case, the purveyor will slice it for you. In that case, ask to be cut about ¼-inch thick, a size good for subsequent chopping and cooking. Many supermarkets also sell chunks of pancetta, ready to cut at home. Be sure to remove the thin plastic casing from the pancetta before cutting. It is easiest to slice if frozen for an hour or two to firm slightly. Use a sharp knife and keep your wits about you (the fat can be slippery) to slice the chunk of pancetta crosswise into ¼-inch-thick rounds, and then into ¼-inch dice.

SOUPS AND SALADS

MINESTRONE

MAKES 6 TO 8 SERVINGS

 inestra *is Italian for "soup," and* minestrone *means a thick soup. With both onions and leeks, and a garden full of vegetables, our version doesn't skimp. It's served in big bowls, and is best with lots of garnishes and a huge slice of bread. Parmesan rind is a surprising, but essential, flavoring—just cut the rind off a big chunk.*

BEANS

⅔ cup dried cannellini (white kidney) beans

1 garlic clove, peeled

1 bay leaf

1 small dried red chile or ¼ teaspoon crushed hot red pepper flakes

1 slice (¼-inch-thick) prosciutto, about 4 ounces, cut into ¼-inch dice (do not trim off the fat)

¼ cup extra-virgin olive oil, plus more for serving

1 large yellow onion, cut into ½-inch dice

1 large leek, white and pale green parts only, cut into ½-inch dice

2 celery ribs, cut into ½-inch dice

2 small carrots, cut into ½-inch dice

4 garlic cloves, minced

1 teaspoon oregano

1 zucchini, trimmed and cut into ½-inch dice

1 can (14.5 ounces) diced tomatoes in juice

1 tablespoon tomato paste

3 cups reduced-sodium chicken broth or water

Rind from a 1-pound chunk of Parmesan cheese, about 6-by-2 inches

1½ cups packed thinly sliced kale or Swiss chard leaves, thick stems removed

Kosher salt and freshly ground black pepper

Basil Pesto (page 139) or store-bought pesto for serving

Freshly grated Parmesan cheese for serving

1. At least 4 hours before cooking the soup, put the beans in a large bowl and add enough water to cover the beans by 2 inches. Let soak for at least 4 hours and up to 8 hours. (Or bring the beans and water to cover by 2 inches to a boil in a medium saucepan over high heat. Boil for 2 minutes. Remove from the heat, cover, and let stand 1 hour.) Drain and rinse the beans.

2. Bring the drained beans, 5 cups water, the garlic, bay leaf, and chile to a boil in a medium saucepan over high heat. Reduce the heat to medium-low and cover with the lid slightly ajar. Simmer until the beans are tender, about 30 minutes, depending on the age of the beans.

3. Cook the prosciutto and oil together in a soup pot over medium heat just until the prosciutto is lightly browned, about 3 minutes. Add the onion and leeks. Cook, stirring occasionally, until softened, about 3 minutes. Add the celery, carrots, garlic, and oregano, and cook until the vegetables are beginning to soften, about 3 minutes more. Add the zucchini and cook until it begins to soften, about 3 minutes.

4. Add the tomatoes and their liquid and the tomato paste, bring to a boil and cook 3 minutes. Add the broth, the beans and their liquid, and the Parmesan rind. Bring to a boil. Reduce the heat to medium-low. Simmer until the flavors are blended, about 1 hour. Stir in the kale and cook until tender, about 5 minutes.

5. Remove the Parmesan rind. Ladle into soup bowls, and top each serving with a spoonful of pesto and a drizzle of oil. Serve hot, with the grated Parmesan cheese passed at the table.

TIP For Beef Minestrone, add 2 pounds beef shanks, browned in a skillet in 2 tablespoons olive oil, to the soup and simmer until the meat is tender, about 2 hours.

PASTA E FAGIOLI

MAKES 6 TO 8 SERVINGS

here are countless ways to make this Italian bean and pasta soup. Many families make it with lentils, but we like it the way Mama Mandola made it with white beans. It's a satisfying, comforting dish that we never get tired of, especially when the weather is chilly. And please: Pronounce it "pasta eh fah-gee-OH-lee," and not "pasta fazool."

1 pound dried cannellini (white kidney) beans

4 ounces sliced (¼-inch-thick) pancetta, cut into ¼-inch dice

2 tablespoons extra-virgin olive oil, plus more for serving

2 ounces (¼-inch-thick) sliced prosciutto, cut into ¼-inch dice

1 medium red onion, chopped

3 celery ribs, cut into ¼-inch dice

4 garlic cloves, minced

1 tablespoon finely chopped fresh rosemary

1¼ teaspoons dried oregano

1 bay leaf

3 cups reduced-sodium chicken broth

1 cup crushed tomatoes

2 cups broken (1-inch lengths) bucatini or soup pasta, such as ditalini

Kosher salt and freshly ground black pepper

Freshly grated Parmesan cheese for serving

1. At least 4 hours before cooking the soup, put the beans in a large bowl and add enough water to cover the beans by 2 inches. Let soak for at least 4 hours and up to 8 hours. (Or bring the beans and water to cover by 2 inches to a boil in a medium saucepan over high heat. Boil for 2 minutes. Remove from the heat, cover, and let stand 1 hour.) Drain and rinse the beans.

2. Cook the pancetta and oil together in a soup pot over medium heat just until the pancetta is lightly browned, about 5 minutes. Using a slotted spoon, transfer the pancetta to paper towels, leaving the fat in the pan. Add the prosciutto and cook, stirring occasionally, until beginning to brown, about 2 minutes. Add the red onion and cook, stirring occasionally, until softened, about 3 minutes. Add the celery until beginning to soften, about 3 minutes more. Add the garlic, rosemary, oregano, and bay leaf and cook, stirring often, until the onion is golden, about 3 minutes.

3. Stir in the broth, crushed tomatoes, drained beans, and the reserved pancetta. Bring to a boil over high heat. Reduce the heat to medium-low and cover with the lid ajar. Simmer, stirring occasionally, until the soup is thick and beans are tender, about 2½ hours, adding water, if needed. Remove the bay leaf.

TIP When beans are cooked with tomatoes, a chemical reaction makes them take a long time to cook, so this soup refuses to be rushed.

4. When the beans are tender, bring a medium saucepan of salted water to a boil over high heat. Add the pasta and stir well. Cook, stirring often, according to the package directions, until the pasta is al dente. Drain well, reserving about 3 cups of the pasta water.

5. Add the pasta to the soup. Stir in enough of the pasta water to give the soup a loose, soupy consistency. Season with salt and pepper. Ladle into soup bowls and drizzle each serving with olive oil. Serve hot, with the Parmesan cheese passed on the side.

3
MEATS

FILET TIPS WITH RED PEPPERS AND ONIONS

eef tenderloin is a great choice for grilling because it doesn't need any marinade to tenderize the meat. If you've been frustrated with undercooked grilled vegetables in the past, you'll love our tip of roasting the vegetables before grilling. You will need eight metal skewers.

2 red bell peppers, seeded and cut into 16 (1½-inch) squares

1 large red onion, separated into layers and cut into 16 (1½-inch) squares

2 tablespoons extra-virgin olive oil

2 pounds beef tenderloin, trimmed, cut into 24 (1½-inch) cubes

2 teaspoons Grill Seasoning (page 146)

1. Preheat the oven to 350°F. Place the bell pepper and red onion squares in a roasting pan and toss with 1 tablespoon of the oil. Cover the pan tightly with aluminum foil. Bake until the vegetables are crisp-tender, about 15 minutes. Uncover and let cool.

2. Prepare an outdoor grill for direct cooking with high heat (see page 6).

3. Have ready 8 metal skewers. For each skewer, alternate 3 filet cubes with 2 bell pepper squares and 2 red onion squares. Brush with the remaining oil and season with the grill seasoning. Let stand at room temperature while the grill heats.

4. Brush the grill grates clean. Place the skewers on the grill. Cook, with the lid closed as much as possible, turning after the first 3 minutes, until the meat is browned, about 6 minutes for medium-rare. Remove from the grill and let stand for 3 minutes.

5. For each serving, slide the meat and vegetables from 2 skewers onto a plate. Serve hot.

TIP Metal skewers are inexpensive and a good investment because, unlike wooden skewers, they are guaranteed not to burn up on the grill.

BEEF FILET WITH BLUE CHEESE SAUCE

MAKES 4 SERVINGS

*B*lue cheese and beef love each other's company. In this recipe, tender grilled beef filet is topped with a pungent sauce. (The sauce is also great with rib-eye steak.) Mashed Potatoes with Mascarpone (page 114) might be the perfect side dish, and plays up the mascarpone in the sauce, too.

BLUE CHEESE SAUCE

½ cup heavy cream

3 ounces (¾ cup) crumbled blue cheese

4 ounces (½ cup) mascarpone cheese

1 teaspoon fresh lemon juice

Kosher salt and freshly ground black pepper

4 filet mignons, cut about 1¼ inches thick, about 5 ounces each

2 tablespoons Grill Baste (page 145) or olive oil

1½ teaspoons Grill Seasoning (page 146)

1. To make the sauce, bring the cream to a simmer in a small saucepan over low heat. Add the blue cheese and whisk until melted and smooth. Whisk in the mascarpone and lemon juice. Season with salt and pepper. Remove from the heat. (The sauce can be made up to 2 hours ahead, stored at room temperature. Reheat, whisking often, over low heat, before serving.)

2. Prepare an outdoor grill for direct cooking over high heat (see page 6).

3. Brush the filets on all sides with the grill baste. Season with the grill seasoning. Let stand at room temperature while the grill heats.

4. Brush the grill grate clean. Lightly oil the grate. Place the beef on the grill. Cook, with the lid closed as much as possible. Turn after 4 minutes. Continue cooking until an instant-read thermometer inserted in the center of a filet reads 125°F for medium-rare, about 4 minutes more.

5. Transfer each filet to a dinner plate. Top with equal amounts of the sauce and serve hot.

TIP You could broil or sauté the filets instead of grilling them. Allow about 4 minutes per side in either case.

PARSLEY-PORK POT ROAST

MAKES 6 TO 8 SERVINGS

low down and take the time to simmer this fall-apart-tender pot roast, a recipe that has been in the family for years. It is even better when served the next day. Serve it with Rosemary Roasted Potatoes and Nonna's Savory Squash Casserole (pages 115 and 118) for a meal that Mama would serve with pride.

1 pork shoulder roast with bones, skin trimmed off, about 4 pounds

8 large garlic cloves, 4 cut into 20 slivers and 4 coarsely chopped

3 tablespoons finely chopped fresh flat-leaf parsley, plus more for serving

Kosher salt and freshly ground black pepper

⅓ cup all-purpose flour

4 tablespoons olive oil, divided

1 small yellow onion, coarsely chopped

1 small carrot, coarsely chopped

1 small celery rib, coarsely chopped

> **TIP** The roast can be made ahead. Carve the roast and place in a baking dish. Add the juices. Cover the dish with aluminum foil. Refrigerate for up to 1 day. Reheat in a 350°F oven until piping hot, about 30 minutes.

1. Preheat the oven to 325°F.

2. Using the tip of a thin-bladed sharp knife, pierce twenty 1-inch-deep slits all around the pork roast. Coat the garlic slivers with the parsley, and insert 1 into each slit. Reserve any remaining parsley. Season the pork with 1½ teaspoons salt and ½ teaspoon pepper. Roll in the flour, shaking off the excess flour.

3. Heat 2 tablespoons of the oil in a large Dutch oven or flameproof casserole over medium-high heat. Add the pork and cook, turning the meat occasionally, adjusting the heat as needed to avoid scorching the flour, until browned, about 10 minutes. Transfer to a plate.

4. Add the remaining 2 tablespoons of oil to the Dutch oven and heat. Add the onion, carrot, and celery and cook, stirring occasionally, until softened, about 3 minutes. Stir in the chopped garlic. Add 2 cups water to the pot and bring to a boil, scraping up the browned bits in the pan with a wooden spoon. Return the pork to the Dutch oven and add the reserved parsley.

5. Cover tightly and bake, turning the pork in the Dutch oven every hour or so, until the meat is fork-tender, about 2½ hours. Transfer to a plate and tent with aluminum foil to keep warm. Let stand for 15 minutes.

6. Strain the cooking liquid into a heatproof bowl, discarding the solids. Let stand for 5 minutes. Skim off the fat from the surface. Season with salt and pepper. Reheat before serving.

7. Carve the pot roast and arrange on a platter. Pour the pan juices on top, sprinkle with parsley, and serve hot.

MEATS

BRAISED SHORT RIBS WITH RED WINE
Beef Brasato

MAKES 6 SERVINGS

 ake this when the mood strikes for a hearty, rib-sticking beef stew. (After all, brasato *means "braised" in Italian.) Raw short ribs, with lots of bone and gristle, don't look promising, but these perceived drawbacks contribute to the succulent sauce. Serve it over Parmesan Risotto (page 116), Garlic Mashed Potatoes (page 111), or plain rigatoni.*

2 tablespoons unsalted butter

1 yellow onion, chopped

1 carrot, chopped

1 celery rib, chopped

2 garlic cloves, chopped

1 cup hearty red wine, such as Citra Montepulciano

2 cups reduced-sodium chicken broth

1 can (14.5 ounces) diced tomatoes in juice

1 tablespoon finely chopped fresh flat-leaf parsley, plus more for garnish

½ teaspoon dried basil

½ teaspoon dried marjoram

½ teaspoon dried rosemary

½ teaspoon dried thyme

Grated zest of ½ lemon

1 bay leaf

6 pounds beef short ribs (preferably meaty individual ribs, also called "English cut," and not cross-cut or flanken)

Kosher salt and freshly ground black pepper

½ cup all-purpose flour

¼ cup olive oil (not extra-virgin)

1. Preheat the oven to 300°F.

2. Melt the butter in a saucepan over medium heat. Add the onion, carrot, celery, and garlic and cook, stirring occasionally, until the onion is translucent, about 5 minutes. Spread the vegetables in a very large roasting pan.

3. Add the wine to the skillet and bring to a boil. Cook until reduced by half, about 3 minutes. Add the broth, tomatoes with their juices, parsley, basil, marjoram, rosemary, thyme, lemon zest, and bay leaf and bring to a boil. Set aside.

4. Season the short ribs with 1 tablespoon salt and 1 teaspoon pepper. Spread the flour in a shallow dish. Roll the ribs in the flour, shaking off the excess flour. Heat the oil in a large skillet over medium-high heat. In batches, add the short ribs and cook,

CARRABBA'S ITALIAN GRILL

36

turning occasionally, until browned on all sides. Arrange the short ribs on the vegetables in the roasting pan. (They can be crowded.)

5. Pour the wine mixture over the short ribs. The liquid should almost cover the short ribs—add water if needed. Place the roasting pan over medium-high heat and bring the liquid to a boil. Remove from the heat and cover the pan tightly with aluminum foil.

6. Bake until the short ribs are fork-tender, about 2¼ hours. Transfer the short ribs to a large serving bowl, discarding the bones. Cover the bowl with aluminum foil to keep the beef warm.

7. Skim off and discard any fat from the surface of the cooking liquid. Bring the liquid to a boil over high heat. Boil, stirring occasionally, until the sauce is reduced and thick enough to coat a wooden spoon, about 15 minutes. Discard the bay leaf. Season with salt and pepper. Pour the sauce over the beef in the bowl. (The beef brasato can be cooled, covered, and refrigerated for up to 3 days. Reheat in the roasting pan, covered with foil, in a preheated 350°F oven until hot, about 45 minutes.) Serve hot.

MEATS

PROSCIUTTO-WRAPPED PORK TENDERLOIN

 his sophisticated entrée is a popular seasonal special at Carrabba's, and we have a hunch that once mastered, it will become your favorite dish for entertaining.

2 pork tenderloins, about 1 pound each, trimmed of fat and silverskin

½ teaspoon Grill Seasoning (page 146)

6 wide slices prosciutto (not paper thin)

2 tablespoons Grill Baste (page 145) or olive oil

PORT WINE AND FIG SAUCE

1 cup tawny port, such as Fairbanks Port

¾ cup reduced-sodium chicken broth

1 Granny Smith apple, unpeeled, cored, and cut into ½-inch dice

¾ cup (½-inch) diced dried figs

1 tablespoon finely chopped yellow onion

6 tablespoons cold unsalted butter, cut into ½-inch cubes

Kosher salt and freshly ground black pepper

1. Prepare an outdoor grill for direct cooking over medium-high heat (see page 6).

2. Season the pork tenderloins with the grill seasoning. Lay 3 prosciutto slices on the work surface with the long sides running vertically and overlapping by about ¼ inch. Place 1 pork tenderloin at a long end of the prosciutto slices and roll the pork up in the prosciutto. Using kitchen twine, tie the tenderloin crosswise in a few places to secure the prosciutto. Repeat with the remaining prosciutto and pork tenderloin. Let stand at room temperature while the grill heats.

3. Meanwhile, start the sauce. Bring the port, stock, apple, figs, and onion to a boil in a medium saucepan over high heat. Boil until the liquid is reduced to about 3 table-spoons, about 10 minutes. Remove from the heat.

4. Brush the grill grate clean. Lightly oil the grill grate. Brush the prosciutto with the grill baste. Put the prosciutto-wrapped tenderloins on the grill. Cook, with the lid closed as much as possible, turning occasionally, until the prosciutto is browned and crisp and an instant-read thermometer inserted in the center of the pork reads 150°F, 15 to 20 minutes. If the prosciutto is browning too quickly, move the tenderloins to the cool part of the grill not over the coals (or reduce the temperature on a gas grill to Low). Transfer to a carving board and let stand for 5 minutes before carving.

5. To finish the sauce, reheat it slightly over high heat. If the fruit has absorbed the liquid, add a tablespoon or two of water to return the liquid to 3 tablespoons. Reduce the heat to very low. A few cubes at a time, whisk in the butter to make a smooth sauce. Season with salt and pepper. Set aside.

TIP If you aren't fond of figs, try dried apricots, although this sauce has converted several fig-haters.

6. Using a thin-bladed knife, remove the twine and cut the tenderloins crosswise into ¾-inch thick slices. Divide the slices evenly among dinner plates, top with the sauce, and serve.

OVEN-ROASTED PORK TENDERLOINS *To cook indoors, brown each prosciutto-wrapped tenderloin in a large nonstick skillet over medium-high heat, about 5 minutes. Transfer to a rimmed baking sheet. Bake in a preheated 375°F oven until an instant-read thermometer inserted in the center reads 150°F, about 20 minutes.*

RIBS AGRODOLCE
Sweet and Sour Ribs

MAKES 4 TO 6 SERVINGS

hese ribs reflect a mix of our Texan and Italian roots. We guarantee that you will love them, even though we are sure that they are nothing like ribs you have enjoyed in the past . . . unless, of course, you ordered them at Carrabba's. The ribs are first braised in red wine, then finished on the grill with a sauce made from the cooking liquid.

5 pounds baby back ribs, cut into 4 slabs

4 teaspoons Grill Seasoning (page 146)

2 tablespoons unsalted butter

1 small yellow onion, coarsely chopped

1 small carrot, coarsely chopped

1 small celery rib, coarsely chopped

2 garlic cloves, minced

Grated zest of ½ lemon

2 cups hearty red wine, such as Citra Montepulciano

2 cups reduced-sodium chicken broth

1 can (14.5 ounces) diced tomatoes in juice

2 tablespoons finely chopped fresh parsley

1 tablespoon finely chopped fresh basil or 1½ teaspoons dried basil

1 teaspoon finely chopped fresh rosemary or ½ teaspoon dried rosemary

1 teaspoon finely chopped fresh thyme or ½ teaspoon dried thyme

½ teaspoon dried marjoram

1 bay leaf

SAUCE

⅓ cup plus 1 tablespoon balsamic vinegar

¼ cup sugar

Kosher salt and freshly ground black pepper

1 scallion, white and green parts, thinly sliced, for garnish

1. Prepare an outdoor grill for direct cooking over high heat (page 6). Or position a broiler rack about 8 inches from the source of heat and preheat the broiler on high.

2. Season the ribs with the grill seasoning. Let stand at room temperature while the grill is heating.

3. Brush the cooking grate clean. Lightly oil the grate. Put the ribs on the grill (or in the broiler). Cook, with the lid closed as much as possible, turning the ribs once, until browned on both sides, about 8 minutes. Or grill the ribs, turning once, until browned, about 10 minutes. Transfer to a large roasting pan. If using a grill, it will have to be reheated later for the final glazing.

4. Preheat the oven to 300°F. Melt the butter in a large skillet over medium heat. Add the onion, carrot, celery, garlic, and lemon zest. Cook, stirring occasionally, until the vegetables soften, about 5 minutes. Add the wine, broth, tomatoes with their juices, parsley, basil, rosemary, thyme, marjoram, and bay leaf. Bring to a boil over high heat. Pour over the ribs in roasting pan. Cover the pan tightly with aluminum foil.

5. Bake until the ribs are tender, about 1¼ hours. Transfer the ribs to a large rimmed baking sheet and let cool.

6. To make the sauce, skim any fat from the surface of the cooking liquid. Discard the bay leaf. In batches, purée the liquid and vegetables in a blender (leave the lid ajar so the steam can escape), and transfer to a bowl. Return the puréed sauce to the roasting pan. Stir in the vinegar and sugar. Bring to a boil over high heat. Cook, stirring often, until reduced by about half and the consistency of barbecue sauce, about 15 minutes. Transfer to a bowl. (The ribs and sauce can be cooled, covered, and refrigerated for up to 1 day ahead.)

7. Prepare an outdoor grill for direct cooking over medium-hot heat (see page 6). Or position a broiler rack about 8 inches from the source of heat and preheat the broiler on high.

8. Brush the cooking grate clean. Lightly oil the grate. Put the ribs on the grill (or in the broiler) Cook, turning occasionally, until browned, about 5 minutes. Brush generously with the sauce and cook, turning occasionally, until glazed, about 5 minutes more. Transfer the ribs to a platter, sprinkle with scallions, and serve.

TIP If you use spareribs, braise them for about 2 hours, until tender.

4
CHICKEN

CHICKEN BRYAN

 ryan is a place, not a person. It is the community where the ancestors of the Carrabba family settled and became cotton farmers after they arrived from Sicily. In honor of our Texan hometown, we've used some our favorite ingredients to create a signature dish that has become a fan favorite.

4 boneless and skinless chicken breast halves, 7 to 8 ounces each

1½ teaspoons Grill Seasoning (page 146)

3 tablespoons Grill Baste (page 145) or olive oil

4 ounces rindless goat cheese log, cut into 8 (¼-inch) rounds

Lemon Butter Sauce (page 140)

4 sun-dried tomatoes packed in oil, drained, and cut lengthwise into ¼-inch-wide strips

1 tablespoon chopped fresh basil, plus more for garnish

1. Prepare an outdoor grill for direct cooking over medium heat (see page 6).

2. Meanwhile, using a flat meat pounder, lightly pound each chicken half to an even thickness of about ½ inch. Cut each breast half in half crosswise to make a total of 8 chicken breast pieces. Season with the grill seasoning. Let stand at room temperature while the grill heats.

3. Brush the grill grate clean. Lightly oil the grate. Brush the chicken on both sides with the grill baste. Cook, with the lid closed as much as possible, turning after 5 minutes, until the chicken is nicely browned and feels firm when the top is pressed with a finger, about 10 minutes total. During the last minute, top each piece with a goat cheese round. Transfer to a platter and tent with aluminum foil to keep warm.

4. Stir the lemon butter sauce in a small saucepan over very low heat with a heatproof spatula just until warm and smooth, but not hot and melted, about 1½ minutes. Stir in the sun-dried tomatoes and basil.

5. Place 2 chicken pieces on each serving plate. Spoon equal amounts of the sauce over each serving, sprinkle with basil, and serve hot.

BROILED CHICKEN BRYAN *Broil the chicken in a preheated broiler with the rack adjusted about 8 inches from the source of heat. Cook, turning occasionally, until firm when pressed with a finger, about 10 minutes. Add the goat cheese about 1 minute before the chicken is done.*

HERB CRUSTED CHICKEN WITH 40 CLOVES OF GARLIC SAUCE

MAKES 4 TO 6 SERVINGS

 here's nothing wrong with plain roast chicken. It's just that it's plain, and at Carrabba's, we're all about flavor. Here's how we make roast chicken, rubbed with lots of herbs, and with a sauce that contains forty cloves of garlic. Don't worry—the garlic is cooked so long that it is as mild as can be.

1 whole chicken, about 5 pounds, giblets and excess fat removed

1 tablespoon extra-virgin olive oil

Kosher salt and freshly ground black pepper

1 tablespoon finely chopped fresh flat-leaf parsley

2 teaspoons finely chopped fresh basil

4 teaspoons finely chopped fresh rosemary, divided

2 cups reduced-sodium chicken broth

1 cup dry white wine, such as Cavit Pinot Grigio

2 tablespoons fresh lemon juice

40 garlic cloves, peeled

1 bay leaf

1. Preheat the oven to 400°F.

2. Rub the chicken with the olive oil. Season the chicken, inside and out, with 2 teaspoons salt and ½ teaspoon pepper. Mix the parsley, basil, and 2 teaspoons of the rosemary. Sprinkle all over the outside of the chicken. Place the chicken, breast side down, on a rack in a roasting pan. Add the broth, wine, lemon juice, garlic, bay leaf, and remaining 2 teaspoons of rosemary to the pan.

3. Roast for 30 minutes. Turn the chicken breast side up and continue roasting (without basting) until the garlic is dark beige and tender, and an instant-read thermometer inserted in the thickest part of the thigh not touching a bone reads 165°F, about 1¼ hours. Transfer the chicken to a carving board. Let stand 10 to 15 minutes before carving.

4. Strain the cooking liquid through a wire sieve into a heatproof bowl and reserve the garlic. Discard the bay leaf. Skim the fat from the surface of the liquid. To make a sauce, in 2 batches, purée the liquid and garlic in a blender with the lid ajar (to allow the steam to escape). Season with salt and pepper.

5. Carve the chicken and serve with the sauce.

PARMESAN-CRUSTED CHICKEN ARUGULA

MAKES 4 SERVINGS

ight and fresh, this lemon-dressed dish reminds us of sunny afternoons on a terrace overlooking the Amalfi Coast. We love Mama's Seasoned Breadcrumbs (page 144), but a few years ago we made room in our hearts for panko, crunchy Japanese-style breadcrumbs. If you have a very large (14-inch) skillet, you can cook all of the breast halves at once.

PARMESAN PANKO

2 cups plain panko

½ cup (2 ounces) freshly grated Romano cheese

½ cup (2 ounces) freshly grated Parmesan cheese

1 teaspoon kosher salt

½ teaspoon freshly ground black pepper

4 boneless and skinless chicken breast halves, 7 to 8 ounces each

1 teaspoon kosher salt

½ teaspoon freshly ground black pepper

3 large eggs, beaten

6 tablespoons olive oil, divided

4 cups baby arugula

1 cup halved grape tomatoes

2 tablespoons fresh lemon juice

Kosher salt and freshly ground black pepper

1 wedge of Parmesan cheese, about 6 ounces, for shaving cheese curls

2 lemons, cut in halves crosswise

1. Preheat the oven to 200°F. Line a rimmed baking sheet with paper towels. Have a second baking sheet nearby.

2. To make the panko, mix the ingredients in a wide, shallow bowl until combined.

3. Using a flat meat pounder, lightly pound each chicken breast half to an even thickness of about ½ inch. Cut each in half crosswise to make a total of 8 chicken breast pieces. Season with the salt and pepper.

4. Beat the eggs in another wide, shallow bowl. Dip the chicken in the eggs, then coat with the panko mixture, patting it to adhere. Place on a platter.

5. Line a baking sheet with paper towels. Heat 3 tablespoons of oil in a large skillet over medium-high heat until the oil is hot and shimmering. Carefully add the chicken. Cook until golden brown, turning after 3 minutes and adjusting the heat as needed

TIP If you have the time, heat up the grill to sear the lemon halves on the cut sides, which warms the fruit to release more juice.

so the chicken cooks steadily without over-browning, about 7 minutes. Using a slotted spatula, transfer to the paper towels to drain briefly. Move to the second baking sheet and keep warm in the oven while frying the remaining chicken. Repeat with the remaining 3 tablespoons of oil and the chicken.

6. Toss the arugula, tomatoes, and lemon juice together in a medium bowl and season with salt and pepper. For each serving, place 2 chicken pieces on each plate, and top each with equal amounts of the salad. Using a swivel vegetable peeler, shave as many Parmesan curls as you like on top. Add the lemon halves and serve immediately.

POLLO ROSA MARIA

ose Marie, Johnny's mother, is the namesake of this chicken dish. Grilled chicken breast is stuffed with two essentials of Italian cooking: fontina cheese and prosciutto. Because the chicken will be stuffed, buy breast halves that are on the large side.

1 tablespoon unsalted butter

10 ounces mushrooms, thinly sliced

4 boneless and skinless chicken breast halves, about 8 ounces each

1 slice prosciutto (not paper-thin), about 1½ ounces, cut into 8 equal pieces

3 ounces fontina cheese, cut into 8 equal slices

2 tablespoons Grill Baste (page 145) or olive oil

1½ teaspoons Grill Seasoning (page 146)

¾ cup Lemon Butter Sauce (page 140)

2 tablespoons coarsely chopped fresh basil

Kosher salt and freshly ground black pepper

1. Prepare an outdoor grill for direct cooking over medium heat (see page 6).

2. Melt the butter in a medium skillet over medium-high heat. Add the mushrooms and cook, stirring occasionally, until lightly browned, about 5 minutes. Set aside.

3. Using a thin-bladed, sharp knife, butterfly each chicken breast: Place a chicken breast on the work surface. Place one hand on the meat to hold it steady. Position a thin-bladed knife at the center of the largest side of the breast half. Make a deep cut through the center of the entire breast half, stopping just before you reach the opposite side, so the breast half can be opened like a book. Cut each breast half in half crosswise at its widest point to make 8 pieces total. Open each piece of chicken, and place 1 piece of each of prosciutto and fontina on the bottom half. Close the chicken, being sure that the filling is enclosed. Brush with the grill baste. Season with the grill seasoning. Let stand at room temperature while the grill heats.

4. Brush the grill grate clean. Lightly oil the grate. Place the chicken on the grill. Cook, with the lid closed as much as possible, turning after 5 minutes, until the chicken is nicely browned and feels firm when the top is pressed with a finger, about 10 minutes total. Transfer to a platter and tent with aluminum foil to keep warm.

5. Reheat the mushrooms over low heat, stirring often. Add the lemon butter sauce and stir just until heated and smooth, about 1½ minutes. Stir in the basil.

6. Place 2 chicken pieces on each serving plate. Spoon equal amounts of the sauce over each serving and serve hot.

BROILED POLLO ROSA MARIA *Broil the chicken in a preheated broiler with the rack adjusted about 8 inches from the source of heat. Cook, turning occasionally, until firm when pressed with a finger, about 10 minutes.*

 Be sure to use dry marsala. Sweet marsala should be reserved for desserts.

CHICKEN MARSALA

MAKES 4 SERVINGS

 staple at Italian restaurants, chicken marsala is usually sautéed. In our grilled version, the breast is topped with a sauce of marsala, mushrooms, and prosciutto. Use the sauce to top grilled veal, steak, or pork chops.

MARSALA SAUCE

3 tablespoons unsalted butter, cut into tablespoons, divided

10 ounces white mushrooms, thinly sliced

2 ounces sliced prosciutto (not paper thin), cut into 2-by-¼-inch strips

3 tablespoons finely chopped yellow onion

1 tablespoon all-purpose flour

¾ cup dry marsala

¾ cup reduced-sodium chicken broth

4 boneless and skinless chicken breast halves, 7 to 8 ounces each

2 tablespoons Grill Baste (page 145) or olive oil

1½ teaspoons Grill Seasoning (page 146)

Finely chopped fresh flat-leaf parsley for garnish

1. To make the sauce, melt 1 tablespoon of the butter in a large skillet over medium-high heat. Add the mushrooms and cook, stirring occasionally, until browned, about 5 minutes. Add the prosciutto and onion and cook, stirring often, until the onion softens, about 2 minutes more. Sprinkle with the flour and stir well. Stir in the marsala and broth and bring to a boil. Cook, stirring often, until reduced to about 1 cup, about 5 minutes. Set aside. (The sauce can be kept at room temperature for up to 2 hours.)

2. Prepare an outdoor grill for direct cooking over medium heat (see page 6).

3. Cut each breast half in half crosswise to make a total of 8 chicken breast pieces. Brush with the grill baste. Season with the grill seasoning.

4. Brush the grill grate clean. Lightly oil the grate. Place the chicken on the grill. Cook, with the lid closed as much as possible, turning after 5 minutes, until the chicken is nicely browned and feels firm when the top is pressed with a finger, about 10 minutes total. Remove from the grill.

5. Reheat the sauce in the skillet over medium heat, stirring constantly. Remove from the heat. One tablespoon at a time, add the remaining butter and stir until incorporated into the sauce. Season with salt and pepper. Place 2 chicken pieces on each serving plate. Spoon equal amounts of the sauce over each serving, sprinkle with parsley, and serve hot.

BROILED CHICKEN MARSALA *Broil the chicken in a preheated broiler with the rack adjusted about 8 inches from the source of heat. Cook, turning occasionally, until firm when pressed with a finger, about 10 minutes.*

CHICKEN

The discovery of a good wine is increasingly better for mankind than the discovery of a new star. —LEONARDO DA VINCI

Sharing delicious wine at the table with friends and loved ones is an integral part of the Italian dining experience, and we continue this delightful practice at Carrabba's. While we profess fondness for the great wines of Italy, such as Chianti, Montepulciano, and Pinot Grigio, we carefully select wines from all over the world to share the spotlight with our food. You'll find wine from California, of course, but also those from regions whose wines are gaining recognition in the global market, such as Argentina and Chile.

Leonardo had it right, and many wines on our list are new discoveries. The Italian house wines you enjoy from our menu are made exclusively for Carrabba's. The Montepulciano d'Abruzzo is produced in the Abruzzo region of Italy. The soft tannins and fruit-forward profile make this a great complement to our red sauces. The crisp, fruity, easy-to-drink Pinot Grigio perfectly complements our lemon butter and Alfredo sauces. Although these wines are not available to the general public, we suggest Citra Montepulciano and Cavit Pinot Grigio as great alternatives.

Buying great wine is only part of the equation—it must be served with appreciation for the time and effort that is put into each bottle. (For wine, like good food, cannot be rushed.) Our waitstaff is carefully trained in all aspects of wine service. Continuing education, in the form of wine tastings and other sessions, ensure that your waitperson can help you choose the right wine for your meal, and that it will be served properly. So, whether it is a glass, a quartino (a glass-and-a-half), or a bottle, the wine is treated with all of the respect it deserves.

GRILLED CHICKEN CARRABBA-STYLE

 any years ago, Johnny's dad got a backyard grill, which came with a basic recipe for grilled chicken. He made a few tweaks, and before long, Mr. C sealed his reputation for cooking the best chicken around. Johnny carries on the family tradition. Cook the chicken over medium heat, apply plenty of layers of Johnny's grill baste, and it will become your family's favorite, too.

1 chicken, about 5 pounds, cut into 2 wings, 2 thighs, 2 drumsticks, and 2 breast halves

2 teaspoons Grill Seasoning (page 146)

¾ cup Grill Baste (page 145)

1. Prepare an outdoor grill for indirect cooking with medium heat (see page 6).

2. Season the chicken pieces with the grill seasoning. Let stand at room temperature while the grill heats.

3. Brush the cooking grate clean. Lightly oil the grate. Brush the chicken well with some of the grill baste. Place on the grill over the foil pan. Cook, with the grill closed as much as possible, turning and basting well with the grill baste every 10 minutes, until an instant-read thermometer, inserted in the thickest part of a breast half, reads 165°F, about 45 minutes. Transfer the chicken to a carving board. Let stand 5 minutes. Chop each breast half in half to make 4 serving pieces, but leave the other pieces intact. Put the chicken on a serving platter and serve hot.

TIP If you have one take-away tip from this recipe, it is this: Cook chicken in a covered grill with indirect medium heat for perfect results.

CHICKEN

5

SEAFOOD

THE CARRABBA'S WAY *Seafood*

We source only the very best seafood at Carrabba's. Maybe it is our founders' Sicilian blood, or maybe it is because they grew up not far from the Gulf of Mexico, but seafood has always held a special place of honor on our menu.

FRESH FISH FILLETS Always buy your fish from a reputable source with a high turnover. Whenever you can, smell the fish, which should have the aroma of the open sea. Fish fillets should be glistening; never buy fish that is iridescent with a rainbow cast. The flesh should be tight, with no gaps.

MUSSELS We use farmed mussels from Prince Edward Island (PEI), Canada. Deliciously plump, so deep purple they are almost black, they are raised in the frigid sea water on ropes to ensure they never touch the sand. Best of all, PEI mussels require minimal cleaning. Wild mussels are very gritty and must be carefully cleaned before use, which is a hassle.

Put PEI mussels in the refrigerator in an opened bag (a closed bag will suffocate them) as soon as you get home, and use within twenty-four hours of purchase. Before cooking, discard any mussels with open, gaping (although if you rap them and they close, they're fine), or cracked shells. Give them a quick rinse under cold running water, and you are ready to cook. To clean wild mussels, pull off the hairy beard from each mussel with pliers, scrub the mussels well under cold running water, and soak them in salted ice water for an hour before draining and rinsing. (We told you they are a hassle!) After cooking, discard mussels with unopened shells.

SHRIMP These shellfish are often identified by place of origin and color. We buy the Gulf Pink variety, which have a sweet flavor and firm texture. There is no national standard for size, and the shrimp size is usually indicated by the number per pound. For example, "21 to 25 count" shrimp means that there are about that number of shrimp per pound. (The label on a bag of this size shrimp might say "21/25 count.") This is a relatively large shrimp perfect for sautées and pasta sauces. For grilling, we use the larger 16/20 shrimp.

SCALLOPS We prefer day-boat scallops, so-called because they are not frozen on the boat (a common practice), and brought in fresh after a single day's fishing. They are also sometimes called "dry" scallops because they are not soaked in the chemical solution that many fisheries use as a preservative.

COD ALLA LIVORNESE

MAKES 4 SERVINGS

ivorno is Tuscany's most vital seaport. The sauce that bears its name is laden with capers and olives, and it is perfect with sweet flaky cod or haddock. But you could really use just about any firm, mild fish or even shrimp or scallops. Linguine or even orzo, tossed with olive oil, would showcase the sauce.

LIVORNESE SAUCE

2 tablespoons extra-virgin olive oil

1 yellow onion, cut into thin half-moons

1 can (28 ounces) whole tomatoes in juice, coarsely crushed (see page 142)

¼ cup coarsely chopped pitted kalamata olives

2 tablespoons drained nonpareil capers

1 teaspoon dried oregano

2 tablespoons extra-virgin olive oil

4 cod or haddock fillets, about 6 ounces each

1 teaspoon Grill Seasoning (page 146)

Kosher salt and freshly ground black pepper

1. To make the sauce, heat the oil in a large saucepan over medium heat. Add the onions and cook, stirring occasionally, until golden brown, about 6 minutes. Add the crushed tomatoes and their juices, olives, capers, and oregano to the saucepan and bring to a simmer. Reduce the heat to medium-low and simmer until the tomato juices thicken and the sauce is slightly reduced, about 20 minutes. Set aside.

2. Heat the oil in a large skillet over medium-high heat. Season the cod with the grill seasoning. Add the cod to the skillet and cook until the underside is golden brown, about 2 minutes. Add the sauce and bring to a simmer. Cook just until the cod is opaque in the center when flaked with the tip of a knife, about 7 minutes. Season with salt and pepper.

3. Using a slotted spatula, transfer each cod fillet to a dinner plate. Top each with equal amounts of the sauce and serve hot.

COZZE IN BIANCO
Mussels in White Sauce

MAKES 4 SERVINGS

 ook these, and you'll be serving a big bowl of glistening mussels in a lemony sauce perfect for dunking big chunks of crusty bread. At Carrabba's, we serve these mussels as an appetizer, but this recipe is dinner-sized. One piece of advice: Buy extra bread!

2 tablespoons extra-virgin olive oil

4 pounds mussels, preferably Prince Edward Island, rinsed

½ cup finely chopped yellow onion

5 garlic cloves, minced

Lemon Butter Sauce (page 140)

¼ cup Pernod or other anise-flavored aperitif

2 tablespoons fresh lemon juice

2 tablespoons chopped fresh basil

1. Heat the oil in a nonreactive pot over medium-high heat. Add the mussels and tightly cover the pot. Cook until the shells are starting to open, about 1 minute. Add the onion and garlic, cover, and shake the pot. Continue cooking until the mussels have opened, about 2 minutes more.

2. Reduce the heat to low. Add the lemon butter sauce, Pernod, lemon juice, and basil and cook, stirring occasionally, until the sauce is hot but not melted, about 30 seconds. Remove from the heat.

3. Using tongs, divide the mussels among 4 deep serving bowls. Pour in equal amounts of the sauce. Serve hot, with an empty bowl to hold the empty shells.

TIP Pernod is an anise-flavored aperitif. French Ricard and domestic Herbsaint are similar. Anisette is too sweet and not a good substitute.

SEARED SCALLOPS WITH SPINACH ORZO

MAKES 4 SERVINGS

*W*hen you need dinner in a hurry, scallops are a great option because they must be cooked quickly for the tastiest results. For this light and flavorful dish, even the tomato sauce, made from quickly roasted grape tomatoes, is speedy. You'll have this simple and classy meal on the table in no time.

BALSAMIC ROASTED TOMATO SAUCE

1 pint grape tomatoes, cut in halves lengthwise

3 tablespoons extra-virgin olive oil, divided

1½ teaspoons balsamic vinegar

Kosher salt and freshly ground black pepper

SPINACH ORZO

1½ cups orzo

1 tablespoon extra-virgin olive oil

2 garlic cloves, thinly sliced

5 ounces baby spinach, rinsed but not dried

Kosher salt and freshly ground black pepper

SCALLOPS

2 tablespoons extra-virgin olive oil

16 sea scallops, rinsed and patted dry with paper towels

½ teaspoon kosher salt

¼ teaspoon freshly ground black pepper

> **TIP** True balsamic vinegar is made only in the Italian provinces of Modena or Emilia Romagna from Trebbiano grapes, which are sweeter than typical wine grapes. We use authentic aged balsamic, made by Modenaceti, which is Italy's best-selling brand.

1. To make the roasted tomato sauce, preheat the oven to 400°F. Toss the tomatoes with 1 tablespoon of the oil on a rimmed baking sheet. Bake until the pan juices look caramelized, about 15 minutes. Transfer to a food processor fitted with the metal chopping blade. Add the vinegar and the remaining 2 tablespoons of the oil and pulse a few times until coarsely chopped. Season with salt and pepper. (The sauce can be made up to 2 hours ahead, kept at room temperature. Reheat in a skillet over medium heat.)

2. To make the spinach orzo, bring a medium saucepan of salted water to a boil over high heat. Stir in the orzo. Cook, stirring often, according the package directions until al dente.

3. About 5 minutes before the orzo is cooked, heat the oil and garlic together in a large saucepan over medium heat until the garlic is softened but not browned, about 3 minutes. Add the spinach with any clinging water and cook, stirring often, until

continues

wilted and tender, about 2 minutes. Drain the orzo well. Add to the spinach and stir. Season with salt and pepper. Cover with the lid ajar to keep warm.

4. To make the scallops, heat the oil in a very large skillet over medium-high heat. Add the scallops, flat side down, and cook until the underside is golden brown, about 2 minutes. Flip the scallops and reduce the heat to medium. Cover and cook until the other sides are golden brown and the scallops are barely opaque throughout, about 3 minutes more.

5. To serve, divide the orzo among 4 serving bowls. Add 4 scallops to each. Top each scallop with equal amounts of the tomato sauce. Serve hot.

"DRUNKEN" TUNA

MAKES 4 SERVINGS

he red wine in the sauce "inebriates" the tuna, but the caramelized onions add plenty of flavor, too. There isn't a tomato in sight with this sauce. You might want to serve it with the Garlic Mashed Potatoes on page 111.

4 tablespoons extra-virgin olive oil, divided

2 medium red onions, cut into thin half-moons

½ teaspoon sugar

2 garlic cloves, minced

1 tablespoon finely chopped fresh flat-leaf parsley

4 tuna steaks, about 8 ounces each

Kosher salt and freshly ground black pepper

1 teaspoon all-purpose flour

1 cup hearty red Italian wine such as Citra Montepulciano

1. Heat 2 tablespoons of the oil in a large skillet over medium heat. Add the onions and sugar. Cook, stirring often, until very tender and caramelized to a deep golden brown, about 20 minutes. Stir in the garlic and parsley and cook until the garlic is fragrant. Transfer the onions to a bowl.

2. Add the remaining 2 tablespoons of oil to the skillet and heat over medium-high heat. Season the tuna with ½ teaspoon salt and ¼ teaspoon pepper. Add to the skillet and cook, turning after 2 minutes, until browned on both sides, about 4 minutes. Transfer to a plate.

3. Return the onions to the skillet. Sprinkle with the flour and stir well. Stir in the wine and bring to a boil. Return the tuna to the skillet, reduce the heat to medium-low, and cover. Simmer until the sauce is lightly thickened but the tuna is still pink in the center when pierced with a sharp knife, about 5 minutes. Transfer the tuna and sauce to dinner plates and serve hot.

SPIEDINO DI MARE

MAKES 4 SERVINGS

t Carrabba's, we use the time-honored Italian trick of breading the seafood before grilling, a step that adds flavor and helps keep the delicate shrimp and scallops moist.

SPIEDINO BREADCRUMBS

2 cups Homemade Plain Breadcrumbs (page 144) or plain dried breadcrumbs

2 tablespoons dried parsley

1 teaspoon granulated garlic

1 teaspoon kosher salt

½ teaspoon freshly ground black pepper

2 tablespoons extra-virgin olive oil

32 jumbo (16/20 count) shrimp, peeled and deveined

32 large sea scallops

1 teaspoon kosher salt

½ teaspoon freshly ground black pepper

8 long wooden skewers, soaked in cold water for at least 30 minutes, drained

2 tablespoons extra-virgin olive oil

Lemon Butter Sauce (page 140), warm

1. Prepare an outdoor grill for direct cooking with medium heat (see page 6).

2. To make the spiedino breadcrumbs, mix the breadcrumbs, parsley, granulated garlic, salt, and pepper together in a large bowl. Stir in the oil, just to moisten the mixture. Spread on a large rimmed baking sheet.

3. Have ready 8 metal skewers. Lightly season the shrimp and scallops with the salt and pepper. On each skewer, alternate 2 shrimp and 2 scallops. Brush with the oil. Roll in the breadcrumbs to lightly coat the seafood.

4. Brush the cooking grate clean. Lightly oil the grate. Place the skewers on the grill. Cook, with the lid closed as much as possible, turning occasionally, until the crumbs are browned and the seafood is opaque, about 8 minutes. Remove from the grill.

5. For each serving, slide the seafood off 2 skewers onto a dinner plate. Spoon equal amounts of the warm lemon butter sauce around the seafood and serve.

BROILED SPIEDINO DI MARE *The skewers can also be cooked in a preheated broiler, with the rack adjusted about 8 inches from the source of heat, turning occasionally, until the crumbs are browned and the seafood is opaque, about 8 minutes.*

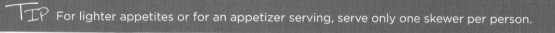
TIP For lighter appetites or for an appetizer serving, serve only one skewer per person.

TROUT ALLA NOCCIOLA

MAKES 4 SERVINGS

occiola *is Italian for "hazelnut," and this rich, flavorful nut is the main flavoring in this excellent seafood entrée. You could try the same coating with other firm fish suitable for grilling, such as snapper. The trick is to use gentle heat so the fish cooks through without scorching the nuts.*

HAZELNUT BREADING

⅔ cup (about 3 ounces) hazelnuts

½ cup Mama's Seasoned Breadcrumbs (page 144) or Italian-style dried breadcrumbs

1 tablespoon extra-virgin olive oil

2 rainbow trout, about 1 pound each, boned by the fish purveyor, with heads and tails removed

½ teaspoon kosher salt

½ teaspoon freshly ground white or black pepper

1 large egg, beaten

Lemon Butter Sauce (page 140)

2 ripe plum (Roma) tomatoes, seeded and cut lengthwise into 8 wedges each

1 tablespoon finely chopped fresh basil

1. To make the hazelnut breading, preheat the oven to 350°F. Spread the hazelnuts on a rimmed baking sheet. Bake, stirring occasionally, until the skins are cracked and the flesh underneath is lightly browned, about 10 minutes. Wrap the hazelnuts in a kitchen towel and let cool for 15 minutes. Rub the nuts in the towel to remove as much skin as possible. Cool completely.

2. Pulse the hazelnuts and breadcrumbs in a food processor fitted with the metal chopping blade about 8 times until the nuts are minced. Transfer to a shallow baking dish. Stir in the oil to make a crumbly, not pasty, mixture.

3. Prepare an outdoor grill for direct cooking with medium heat (see page 6).

4. Open each filleted trout, like a book, and cut each in half crosswise to make 4 portions. Season with the salt and pepper. Beat the egg in a shallow baking dish. Dip each trout portion in the egg, and then the hazelnut breading, patting on the breading to help it adhere.

5. Brush the grill grate clean. Lightly oil the grate. Place the fillets on the grate. Cook, with the lid closed as much as possible, until the underside is lightly browned, about 2 minutes. Flip the fillets and cook for 2 minutes longer. Move the fish to the edges of a charcoal grill not directly over the coals, or reduce the temperature of a gas grill to

TIP Don't worry about getting every last bit of skin off the hazelnuts, as it adds flavor and color. You can also purchase skinned hazelnuts and toast them as above.

low. Continue cooking until the fish is opaque in the center when pierced with the tip of a sharp knife, 2 to 3 minutes more. Transfer to a platter.

6. Stir the lemon butter sauce, tomatoes, and basil in a small skillet over low heat until the sauce is smooth and warm, but not melted and hot, about 1½ minutes. Transfer each trout portion to a dinner plate, and spoon the sauce on top. Serve hot.

BROILED TROUT ALLA NOCCIOLA *To grill the trout, position a broiler rack about 8 inches from the source of heat and preheat the broiler to high. Reduce the heat to medium. Place the trout in a broiler pan. Broil until the nuts are lightly toasted, about 3 minutes. Turn carefully, and continue broiling until the fish is opaque in the center when pierced with the tip of a sharp knife, about 3 minutes more.*

SEAFOOD

69

6

PASTA

THE CARRABBA'S WAY *Pasta*

We boil up tons of pasta every week at Carrabba's. Pasta, a staple in American homes as much as it is in restaurants, is one of those foods you might take for granted. Here are some tips to turn a good bowl of pasta into a *great* one.

- Carefully match the pasta to the sauce. Fresh pasta, made from eggs and flour, has a delicate texture that goes best with light-bodied, gently seasoned sauces. We use fresh fettuccine, tagliatelle, and lasagne. (If you are used to lasagne with dried noodles, our fresh pasta version on page 74 will be an eye-opener.) Our delicious stuffed pastas are made by Joseph's Pasta. When we first started working with Joe Faro, it was a little company, and now it is highly regarded as a national pasta purveyor. Joe worked closely with us to get our famous lobster ravioli just right, with chunks of identifiable lobster in the filling instead of the ground-up mystery seafood found elsewhere. It's an example of how we like to work closely with our purveyors to "try, try again" until we reach perfection.

- On the other hand, dried pasta, usually created from semolina (a coarse grind of durum wheat) and water, will stand up to thicker sauces that are more boldly seasoned. When using dried pasta, go Italian. The best Italian pasta companies use machines with brass dies. The tiny irregularities in the dies transfers to the pasta surface, and this rough exterior makes the sauce cling better. Many American companies use Teflon or stainless steel dies, which make smooth pasta that doesn't hold the sauce as well. Our favorite dried pasta, the one that we have cooked with for years, is Garafolo, made in a little hill town in Sicily. They've been in business for over two hundred years. A lot of guests compliment its firm texture and full flavor ... and we agree. You may not find it at your supermarket, but some sites sell it online.

- Choose the right pot. Use a thin-gauge metal pot so the burner heat can transfer quickly to the water for faster heating.

- Don't crowd the pasta: Pasta loves to swim. Allow 1 gallon of water for every pound of pasta. With most home cookware, it is hard to cook more than a single pound at a time. If you have a stock pot, you might be able to cook 2 pounds at once, but that's it.

- Bring the water to a full boil before adding the salt. Salt dissolves more readily in hot water. Undissolved salt in the bottom of the pot can cause pitting in metal. How much salt to use? Use enough to make the water taste salty. If you are the kind of person who insists on measuring, that's 2 tablespoons of salt to every 1 gallon of water.

- To keep the pasta from sticking together, don't just dump the pasta into the water. As soon as it is added, give it a good stir to be sure it isn't clumping. This is especially important with long pasta strands like spaghetti and linguine. Do not believe the advice to add oil to the water to discourage sticking. It doesn't work. What it does do, however, is slick the pasta so when it is drained and tossed with sauce, the sauce slides right off.

- The only way to really tell when pasta is done is to steal a piece from the pot and taste it. It should be *al dente,* or "to the tooth." You should see the tiniest speck of white in the center of the bitten pasta. Because the timing changes from brand to brand, we recommend that you follow the package directions for how long to cook your pasta.

- After draining the pasta, shake it well in the colander to remove the excess water. Never oil or rinse cooked pasta. Both of these no-nos will keep the sauce from "marrying" the pasta. (Okay, you might want to rinse pasta for cold pasta salad and rinse and oil lasagne noodles so they don't stick together.)

- Return the drained pasta to the pot you cooked it in. The retained heat of the pot will keep the pasta hot when you toss it with the sauce. Preheat your serving dish by adding hot tap water to the dish and letting it stand for a few minutes until warm, then drain and dry the dish.

- Use the right serving utensil for the kind of pasta you are dishing up. Long pasta can be handled with a two-prong meat fork or tongs. Short pasta is easiest to serve with a ladle or large utility spoon. Stuffed pasta, like ravioli, calls for the utility spoon.

LASAGNE

ur recipe for lasagne is stripped to its essentials—fresh pasta, three cheeses, meat, and tomato sauce. You will see recipes that are longer, but few that are better, or made with more love and care. You can substitute 15 dried lasagne noodles, cooked according to the package directions, for the 5 pasta sheets. Use 3 noodles, overlapping as needed, for each layer of lasagne.

Olive oil for the baking pan and lasagne sheets

1½ pounds sweet or hot Italian sausage, casings removed, or ground round beef (85% lean)

5 fresh lasagne sheets

About 7 cups Marinara Sauce (page 141)

2 cups (8 ounces) freshly grated Parmesan cheese, plus more for serving

1 pound (4 cups) shredded part-skim mozzarella

1½ pounds whole milk or part-skim ricotta cheese

Finely chopped fresh flat-leaf parsley for serving

1. Preheat the oven to 350°F. Lightly oil a 13-by-9-inch baking pan.

2. Cook the sausage in a large skillet over medium heat, breaking up the sausage well with the side of a spoon, until cooked through, about 10 minutes. Using a slotted spoon, transfer the sausage to a bowl, discarding the fat in the skillet. Set aside.

3. Bring a large pot of water to a boil over high heat. Add salt to taste. Trim the lasagne sheets to fit the baking pan, if necessary. Add the lasagne sheets, one at a time, stirring gently to keep the sheets from sticking to each other. Cook just until al dente, about 2 minutes (the water does not have to return to a boil). Drain and rinse under cold running water. Separate and toss the lasagne sheets with 2 tablespoons of oil to discourage sticking.

4. Set aside ½ cup of Parmesan cheese for the topping. Spread ¾ cup of the sauce on the bottom of the baking dish. Top with 1 lasagne sheet. Sprinkle with one-quarter each of the mozzarella, Parmesan, and sausage, dot with one-quarter of the ricotta, and top with ¾ cup of marinara sauce. Repeat three times with 3 more sheets, the mozzarella, Parmesan, sausage, ricotta, and marinara sauce. Top with the final lasagne sheet, 1 cup marinara sauce, and the reserved Parmesan cheese. Cover loosely with aluminum foil. Reserve the remaining marinara sauce. (The lasagne and sauce can be prepared, covered, and refrigerated, up to 1 day ahead.)

5. Put the baking dish on a rimmed baking sheet. Bake for 45 minutes. Uncover and bake until the lasagne is bubbling, about 30 minutes more. Let stand for 15 minutes before serving.

6. To serve, reheat the remaining marinara sauce. Cut the lasagne into 9 portions. Transfer each to a dinner plate, top with marinara sauce, and sprinkle with Parmesan and parsley.

 This recipe uses 7 cups of Marinara Sauce (page 141). Make a double batch of that recipe and reserve the remaining sauce for another use.

LINGUINE PESCATORE

 escatore is a tomato-based seafood sauce (pescatore means "fisherman-style") that goes right back to our Sicilian roots. For such a sauce, the seafood must be top-notch, and we source only the best so every bite is a sweet and briny treat. Use large shrimp and scallops so they finish cooking at the same time. If they are too small, they may overcook by the time the mussels open.

1 pound dried linguine
Marinara Sauce (page 141)
12 jumbo (16/20) shrimp, peeled and deveined
12 large sea scallops
24 mussels, preferably Prince Edward Island, rinsed
Kosher salt and freshly ground black pepper

1. Bring a large pot of water to a boil over high heat. Add salt to taste. Add the linguine and stir well to be sure the strands are separated. Cook according to the package directions, stirring occasionally, until al dente.

2. Time the sauce so it is done about the same time as the pasta. Heat the marinara sauce in a large saucepan over medium-high heat, stirring often, until simmering. Add the shrimp, scallops, and mussels and cover the saucepan tightly. Cook until the mussels have opened and the shrimp and scallops are firm and opaque, about 5 minutes. Season with salt and pepper. Using tongs, transfer the mussels to a bowl.

3. When the linguine is done, drain it well. Return it to its cooking pot, pour in the seafood sauce, and mix well. Using tongs, divide the linguine, and then the mussels among serving bowls. Serve hot.

TIP You hear a lot of Italian cooking experts say to never serve grated cheese with seafood. We say, if you like it, go for it.

LOBSTER MACARONI AND CHEESE

W hile Carrabba's heart and soul are in sharing our family recipes, there are a few more indulgent dishes on the menu that are appropriate for very special occasions. For example, this luxurious lobster pasta dish that we guarantee is not your family's mac and cheese—not that there is anything wrong with that!

LOBSTER AND STOCK

Two 1¼-pound lobsters, cooked at the market

One 8-ounce bottle clam juice

½ cup coarsely chopped onion

1 celery rib, thinly sliced

¼ cup dry white wine, such as Cavit Pinot Grigio

LOBSTER SAUCE

2 tablespoons unsalted butter

2 ounces pancetta, cut into ¼-inch dice

½ cup finely chopped yellow onion

½ cup dry white wine, such as Cavit Pinot Grigio

1¼ cups heavy cream

2 cups (8 ounces) shredded fontina cheese

2 ounces rindless goat cheese, crumbled

¼ cup freshly grated Romano cheese

Kosher salt

Crushed hot red pepper flakes

1 pound cavatappi or fusilli

8 tablespoons Mama's Seasoned Breadcrumbs (page 144) for serving

1. To make the stock, remove the lobster meat from the shells, discarding the viscera. Cut the lobster meat into bite-sized pieces, transfer to bowl, cover and refrigerate until serving. Using a heavy knife or cleaver, coarsely chop the lobster shells. Bring the shells, 3½ cups water, clam juice, onion, celery, and wine to a boil in a medium saucepan over high heat. Reduce the heat to medium-low and simmer until reduced to 3 cups, about 30 minutes. Strain the stock into a heatproof bowl; discard the solids.

2. To make the sauce, melt the butter in a medium saucepan over medium heat. Add the pancetta and cook, stirring occasionally, until lightly browned, about 5 minutes. Add the onion and cook, stirring occasionally, until golden, about 5 minutes. Increase the heat to high. Add the wine and bring to a boil, scraping up any browned bits in the saucepan with a wooden spoon. Add the stock, bring to a boil, and cook until reduced by half, about 15 minutes. Add the cream, bring to a boil, and cook until lightly thickened,

about 5 minutes. Reduce the heat to low. (The sauce can be made up to 8 hours ahead, cooled, covered, and refrigerated. Reheat in the saucepan over low heat before using.)

3. Bring a large pot of water to a boil over high heat. Add salt to taste. Add the pasta and stir well. Cook, stirring occasionally, according to the package directions until al dente. Drain well and return the pasta to its cooking pot.

4. Just before the pasta is done, add the lobster meat to the sauce and cook until heated, about 1 minute. Add the fontina, goat, and Romano cheeses and stir until melted. Season with salt and hot red pepper. Add to the pasta and mix well. Divide among 4 serving bowls and sprinkle each with 2 tablespoons of the breadcrumbs. Serve hot.

MAMA MANDOLA'S MEATBALLS WITH SPAGHETTI AND TOMATO SAUCE

MAKES 36 MEATBALLS, ENOUGH FOR 12 SERVINGS

 nother family heirloom recipe that has found its way onto Carrabba's menu, these meatballs will melt in your mouth. We recommend making and freezing a big batch, then using them as required because it is difficult to cook more than one pound of pasta at a time.

MEATBALLS

Olive oil for the baking sheets

1 cup coarsely chopped yellow onion

2 scallions, white and green parts, coarsely chopped

¼ cup coarsely chopped fresh flat-leaf parsley

¼ cup coarsely chopped fresh basil

1 garlic clove

1 large egg, beaten

½ cup Homemade Plain Breadcrumbs (page 144) or plain dried breadcrumbs

½ cup freshly grated Romano cheese

4 teaspoons kosher salt

½ teaspoon freshly ground black pepper

1¾ pounds ground round beef (85% lean)

1¾ pounds ground pork

1 quart Tomato Sauce "Pomodoro" (page 143)

12 Mama Mandola's Meatballs

1 pound dried spaghetti, cooked and drained (see page 72)

Freshly grated Romano cheese for serving

1. Position racks in the top third and center of the oven and preheat the oven to 375°F. Lightly oil 2 large rimmed baking sheets.

2. Pulse the onion, scallions, parsley, basil, and garlic together in a food processor fitted with the metal blade about 8 times, or until very finely minced. Add the egg and pulse a few times to combine. Transfer to a large bowl.

3. Add ¾ cup of water, the breadcrumbs, Romano cheese, salt, and pepper and stir to combine. Add the ground round and ground pork and mix well. Using hands rinsed under cold water, shape the mixture into 36 meatballs. Arrange the meatballs on the baking sheets.

4. Bake until the meatballs are browned and show no sign of pink when pierced with the tip of a knife, about 25 minutes. Let cool. (The meatballs can be transferred to an airtight container and frozen for up to 2 months. Thaw overnight in the refrigerator before using.)

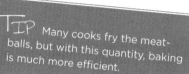
TIP Many cooks fry the meatballs, but with this quantity, baking is much more efficient.

5. For each pound of pasta, combine 1 quart of tomato sauce and ½ cup of water in a large saucepan. Add 12 meatballs and bring to a simmer. Cook, stirring occasionally, taking care not to break up the meatballs, until the meatballs are heated through and the sauce is slightly reduced, about 20 minutes.

6. Using a slotted spoon, transfer the meatballs to a bowl. Add the sauce to the hot spaghetti and mix well. Using tongs, transfer the spaghetti to 4 serving bowls. Top each with 3 meatballs. Serve hot, with the Romano cheese passed on the side.

CAVATAPPI AMATRICIANA

 matriche, a town east of Rome, is the birthplace of this zesty tomato sauce. You can tell that it is from "northern" Italy and not Sicily because it uses butter instead of olive oil and skips the garlic. While this recipe is for dinner-sized portions, Cavatappi Amatriciana is one of our most popular side dishes, and is a perfect match for our grilled dishes.

AMATRICIANA SAUCE

3 tablespoons unsalted butter, divided

4 ounces pancetta, cut into ½-inch dice

1 yellow onion, finely chopped

1 can (28 ounces) whole tomatoes in juice, crushed (see page 142)

½ teaspoon crushed hot red pepper flakes

Kosher salt

1 pound cavatappi or fusilli pasta

½ cup freshly grated Romano cheese, plus more for serving

1. To make the amatriciana sauce, melt 1 tablespoon of the butter in a large saucepan over medium heat. Add the pancetta and cook, stirring occasionally, until lightly browned, about 5 minutes. Add the onion and cook, stirring occasionally, until a rich golden color, about 8 minutes.

2. Stir in the tomatoes and their juices, 1 cup water, and the hot pepper flakes. Bring to a boil. Reduce the heat to medium-low and simmer, stirring occasionally, until the tomato juices have thickened, about 20 minutes. Remove from the heat and stir in the remaining 2 tablespoons of butter until absorbed into the sauce. Season with the salt.

3. Meanwhile, bring a large pot of water to a boil over high heat. Add salt to taste. Add the cavatappi and stir well. Cook, stirring occasionally, according to the package directions until al dente.

4. Drain well and return the cavatappi to its cooking pot. Add the sauce and Romano cheese and stir well. Divide among 4 serving bowls. Serve hot, with additional Romano cheese passed on the side.

TIP Buy pancetta in a 1-pound chunk and cut in thick slices as needed. Refrigerate for 5 days or freeze for up to 2 months. Be sure to remove any plastic casing before using.

PASTA CARRABBA

talian cooks know that when you use good ingredients, the result is bigger than the sum of its parts. This pasta dish is just sautéed mushrooms with peas in a creamy sauce, tossed with grilled chicken breast. But when the chicken breast is carefully seasoned and the entire dish is cooked with care, this is pasta worthy of the Carrabba name.

2 boneless and skinless chicken breast halves, about 8 ounces each, pounded with a flat meat pounder to ½-inch thickness

1½ teaspoons Grill Seasoning (page 146)

2 tablespoons Grill Baste (page 145), or olive oil

1 tablespoon extra-virgin olive oil

10 ounces white mushrooms, thinly sliced

2 garlic cloves, minced

2 cups Alfredo Sauce (page 138)

½ cup frozen peas, thawed

Kosher salt and freshly ground black pepper

1 pound fresh fettuccine

½ cup (2 ounces) freshly grated Romano cheese, plus more for serving

Chopped fresh flat-leaf parsley for garnish

1. Prepare an outdoor grill for direct cooking with medium heat (see page 6). Bring a large pot of water to a boil over high heat. Add salt to taste.

2. Season the chicken breast halves with the grill seasoning, and brush on both sides with the grill baste. Let stand at room temperature while the grill heats.

3. Brush the grill grate clean. Lightly oil the grate. Put the chicken on the grill. Cook, with the lid closed as much as possible, until the chicken feels firm when pressed on top, about 10 minutes. Transfer to a carving board and let stand while making the sauce and cooking the pasta.

4. Heat the oil over medium-high heat in a large skillet. Add the mushrooms and cook, stirring occasionally, until the mushrooms are lightly browned, about 5 minutes. Add the garlic and cook until fragrant, about 30 seconds. Add the Alfredo sauce and peas and bring to a simmer. Cut the chicken across the grain into ½-inch thick slices and add to the skillet. Season with salt and pepper. Remove from the heat.

5. Add the fettuccine to the boiling water. Stir well to separate the strands. Cook, stirring occasionally, according to the package directions, until al dente. Drain well.

6. Return the fettuccine to its cooking pot. Add the sauce and Romano cheese and toss with tongs until the pasta is nicely coated. Divide the pasta among 4 serving bowls.

PASTA

PASTA RAMBO

o, this is not named after a Sylvester Stallone movie. One night at our Kirby location, a line cook, Rambo, created this pasta dish with shrimp and vegetables, with lemon butter sauce. We cooked over a hundred orders that night alone. Pasta Rambo is now a Carrabba's classic.

1 pound dried linguine

2 tablespoons extra-virgin olive oil, divided

10 ounces white mushrooms, sliced

1 pound medium (21/25 count) shrimp, peeled and deveined

5 ounces (4 packed cups) fresh spinach leaves, washed well, stems removed, and coarsely chopped

2 ripe plum (Roma) tomatoes, seeded and cut into ½-inch dice

Lemon Butter Sauce (page 140)

2 tablespoons coarsely chopped fresh basil

Kosher salt and freshly ground white pepper

1. Bring a large pot of water to a boil over high heat. Add salt to taste. Add the linguine and stir well to separate the strands. Cook according to the package directions until al dente.

2. Meanwhile, move fast to make the sauce, which you want to be finished at the same time as the pasta. Heat 1 tablespoon of the oil in a very large skillet over medium-high heat. Add the mushrooms and cook, stirring occasionally, until tender, about 5 minutes. Transfer to a bowl.

3. Heat the remaining tablespoon of oil in the skillet. Add the shrimp and cook, stirring occasionally, until barely opaque around the edges, about 1½ minutes. Add the spinach and cook until wilted, about 1 minute. Stir in the tomatoes and cook until heated, about 1 minute. Return the mushrooms to the pan. Stir in the lemon butter sauce and basil and reduce the heat to low. Stir over very low heat just until the sauce is warmed and smooth, and not hot and melted, about 30 seconds. Season with salt and white pepper.

4. Drain the pasta well and return to the cooking pot. Add the sauce and mix well. Using tongs, transfer the pasta to 4 warm bowls and serve immediately.

PENNE FRANCO

MAKES 4 SERVINGS

 ou will be happy to eat your veggies with this pasta dish, named for a longtime line cook at the original Carrabba's. This is another meal in minutes that can be prepared in the time it takes for the pasta to cook.

1 pound dried penne

2 tablespoons extra-virgin olive oil

10 ounces white mushrooms, thinly sliced

4 garlic cloves, minced

12 drained sun-dried tomatoes in oil, cut into ¼-inch-wide strips

1 package (10 ounces) frozen artichoke hearts, thawed and coarsely chopped,
or 1 cup drained, rinsed, and coarsely chopped canned artichoke hearts

½ cup pitted and coarsely chopped kalamata olives

1 tablespoon finely chopped flat-leaf parsley

8 tablespoons freshly shredded ricotta salata cheese, plus more for serving

1. Bring a large pot of water to a boil over high heat. Add salt to taste. Add the penne and stir well. Cook, stirring occasionally, according to the package directions, until al dente.

2. Meanwhile, move fast to make the sauce, which you want to be finished at the same time as the pasta. Heat the oil in a very large skillet over medium-high heat. Add the mushrooms and cook, stirring occasionally, until tender, about 5 minutes. Add the garlic and cook until fragrant, about 1 minute. Add the sun-dried tomatoes, artichokes hearts, and olives and cook, stirring often, until hot, about 2 minutes more. Set aside.

3. Drain the penne well and return to its cooking pot. Add the vegetable mixture and parsley and stir well. Divide the pasta among 4 serving bowls. Sprinkle each with 2 tablespoons of ricotta salata and serve hot, with additional shredded ricotta salata passed on the side.

PASTA

PASTA WEESIE

MAKES 4 SERVINGS

 ohnny's sister Mary Louise has a nickname: Weesie. Here is "her" pasta, with two sauces to really deliver a bowl full of flavor. Make the sauces ahead of time, and the dish will come together in no time at all.

2 tablespoons extra-virgin olive oil, divided

10 ounces white mushrooms, sliced

1 pound medium (21/25 count) shrimp, peeled and deveined

2 garlic cloves, minced

Lemon Butter Sauce (page 140)

2 scallions, white and green parts, thinly sliced

Kosher salt and freshly ground white pepper

1 pound fresh fettuccine

2 cups Alfredo Sauce (page 138)

½ cup freshly grated Romano cheese, plus more for serving

1. Bring a large pot of water to a boil over high heat. Add salt to taste.

2. Meanwhile, move fast to make the sauce, which you want to be finished at the same time as the pasta. Heat 1 tablespoon of the oil in a very large skillet over medium-high heat. Add the mushrooms and cook, stirring occasionally, until tender, about 5 minutes. Transfer to a bowl.

3. Heat the remaining tablespoon of oil in the skillet. Add the shrimp and cook, stirring occasionally, until almost opaque throughout, about 3 minutes. Add the garlic and cook, stirring occasionally, until the garlic softens, about 1 minute more. Return the mushrooms to the pan. Stir in the lemon butter sauce and scallions and reduce the heat to very low. Stir just until the sauce is warmed and smooth, but not hot and melted, about 30 seconds. Season with salt and white pepper. Set aside.

4. Add the fettuccine to the boiling water and stir well to separate the strands. Cook according to the package directions until al dente. Drain well and return to the cooking pot. Add the Alfredo sauce and Romano cheese and mix well.

5. Using tongs, transfer the pasta to 4 warm bowls. Top with equal amounts of the shrimp mixture and serve immediately, with additional Romano passed at the table.

RIGATONI AL FORNO

 here are few dishes that will make your mouth water more quickly than a hot and bubbling dish of baked pasta. This casserole of pasta, meat, cheese, and tomato sauce—with minor variations, of course—is in every Italian cook's repertory. Remember that the pasta will be baked in the oven, so don't overcook it in the initial boiling.

Olive oil for the baking dish

1 pound sweet or hot Italian sausage, casings removed

1 quart Marinara Sauce (page 141)

1 pound dried rigatoni or other tube-shaped pasta

2 cups (8 ounces) shredded mozzarella cheese

½ cup (2 ounces) freshly grated Parmesan cheese

1 cup whole milk or part-skim ricotta cheese

1. Preheat the oven to 350°F. Bring a large pot of water to a boil over high heat. Add salt to taste. Lightly oil a 13-by-9-inch baking dish.

2. Cook the sausage in a large skillet over medium heat, breaking up the sausage with the side of a spoon, until cooked through, about 10 minutes. Pour off the excess fat. Stir the marinara sauce and bring to a simmer.

3. Meanwhile, add the rigatoni to the water and stir well. Cook according to the package directions, stirring occasionally, until the rigatoni is very al dente. Drain well. Return the rigatoni to its cooking pot. Add the marinara mixture, mozzarella, and Parmesan and stir to combine.

4. Spread the rigatoni mixture in the baking dish. Top with 8 equally placed dollops of ricotta. Bake until bubbling and the ricotta is lightly browned, about 20 minutes. Let stand for 5 minutes. Serve hot, being sure each serving has the ricotta on top.

> TIP Make this a vegetarian dish by substituting 1 pound of sautéed white mushrooms for the sausage.

TAGLIARINI WITH PICCHI PACCHIU SAUCE

MAKES 4 SERVINGS

T *his is the full name of the menu item "Tag Pic Pac." We had to shorten it because so few customers felt comfortable pronouncing* picchi pacchiu *(peek-ee pock-ee-oo). In Sicily,* picchi pacchiu *is what cooks make for a quick tomato sauce with a minimum of cooking. Some cooks use raw garlic, but we prefer to cook it lightly to tame its flavor a bit.*

PICCHI PACCHIU SAUCE

½ cup extra-virgin olive oil

4 garlic cloves, thinly sliced

1 can (28 ounces) whole tomatoes in juice

½ cup chopped fresh basil

Kosher salt and freshly ground black pepper

1 pound fresh tagliarini or fettuccine

1. To make the sauce, heat the oil and garlic together in a small skillet over medium-low heat just so the garlic is softened and the oil is very warm, about 5 minutes. Remove from the heat and let stand to infuse the oil, about 30 minutes.

2. Pour the tomatoes and their juices into a bowl. Squeeze the tomatoes through your fingers until they are coarsely crushed. Stir in the garlic in its oil and the basil. Season with salt and pepper. Let stand for 1 to 2 hours for the flavors to marry.

3. Bring a large pot of water to a boil over high heat. Add salt to taste. Add the tagliarini and stir well to separate the strands. Cook according to the manufacturer's directions until al dente. Drain well.

4. Return the tagliarini to its cooking pot. Add the sauce and mix well. Cover and let stand for 1 minute. Divide among 4 serving bowls and serve hot.

TIP When local tomatoes are in season, use 3 pounds ripe plum (Roma) tomatoes, peeled, seeded, and cut into ½-inch dice, instead of canned tomatoes.

7

PIZZA

THE CARRABBA'S WAY *Pizza*

Our wood-fired pizza is just one reason why so many of Carrabba's *amici* (Italian for "friends," and our affectionate term for our regular customers) return again and again. Only the most dedicated cooks have wood-burning ovens at home, but you can re-create our crisp crust and mouthwatering flavor combinations at home.

- You will need a couple of basic pizza-making tools, available at kitchenware stores and online.

    A baking stone for the oven gives the pizza dough a hot, flat surface for browning. Get the largest size your oven will hold, preferably at least 14 inches square or round.

    A paddle-shaped wooden pizza peel is needed to transfer the pizza in and out of the oven. Our pizza recipes make 12-inch round pizzas, so the paddle area of the peel should be at least 12 inches square.

- If you check out a pizza master at work, a rolling pin is never used to shape the dough. Instead, the dough is patted, pulled, and stretched into a round. The secret here is the dough itself. Gluten is the component in flour that gives a dough structure. Dough made with high-gluten flour, such as bread flour, will spring back during shaping and be hard to work with. We've developed dough with unbleached all-purpose flour that is perfect for home use and easy to shape. It makes a tasty, crisp dough with lots of air bubbles.

- A very high oven temperature will quickly brown the crust and give character to your homemade pizza. Place the stone in the oven on the lowest rack. Turn on the oven and allow at least 30 minutes to reach 550°F. Very large baking stones may inhibit the oven's heat circulation and slow preheating. In that case, preheat without the stone to 550°F, add the stone and let it heat for 20 to 30 minutes.

- To shape the dough, after rising, turn it out onto a lightly floured work surface. Don't punch it down—you want to keep the air in the dough as much as possible. Using floured hands, pat, press, and shape it into a 9-inch-diameter round. Pick up the dough and drape it over one floured hand, clenched in a fist. Clench your other floured hand into a fist, and put it under the dough next to the first fist. Work your fists around the perimeter of the dough, moving them apart a few inches as the dough rotates, gently stretching the edge of the dough to widen the round. Let the dough hang down in front of your fists so gravity can do some of the stretching. By the time you make a full rotation, the dough will have stretched to 12 inches or so. Lay the dough on the floured work surface to check the diameter, thickness, and shaping, and make adjustments by patting and stretching as necessary.

- The next step is to move the dough to the peel. Evenly sprinkle about 2 tablespoons of semolina (a coarse grind of durum wheat), cornmeal, or whole wheat flour over the pizza peel. The layer should be fairly thick to act as a buffer so the pizza can easily slide off the peel and onto the hot stone. Slide the dough from the work surface onto the peel, and reshape it as necessary.

- Add the toppings directly on the dough on the peel. Brushing the dough with oil acts as a barrier to keep the dough from getting soggy from the ingredients. Be judicious with the toppings. Too many ingredients, especially high-moisture ones, will lead to droopy pizza.

- When the toppings are in place, move the pizza to the oven. Shake the peel gently to be sure that the pizza slides and is not sticking. Working quickly, open the oven door and put the peel with the pizza inside. Position the far end of the peel toward the rear of the pizza stone. Using a quick jerking motion, slide the pizza off the peel and onto the stone. Close the door immediately and bake according to the recipe directions, or until the underside of the crust is golden brown (use the peel to lift up and check the color), about 8 minutes.

- To serve, slip the peel under the pizza and remove it from the oven. Transfer to a large chopping board. Let stand for a few minutes to slightly cool before cutting into wedges with a pizza wheel.

PIZZA DOUGH

 reat pizza begins with great dough. We've simplified this dough by using instant yeast to avoid worrying about water temperature, and provided two ways to make it according to your kitchen equipment. Note that you will adjust the amount of flour or water depending on the method you choose. Nothing is set in stone when it comes to yeast baking, as the humidity in the air (and flour) affects the required amount of water.

⅔ cup water

1 tablespoon extra-virgin olive oil, plus more for the bowl

1 teaspoon salt (fine sea, table, iodized, or plain, not kosher)

1 teaspoon instant (also called bread-machine or quick-rise) yeast

2 cups unbleached all-purpose flour, as needed

Olive oil for the bowl

1. **To make the dough in a heavy-duty standing mixer,** combine the water, oil, salt, and yeast in the bowl of the mixer fitted with the paddle attachment. With the machine on low, gradually add enough of the flour to make a soft dough that pulls away from the sides of the bowl. Change to the dough hook. Knead on medium-low speed, adding more flour as needed to keep the dough tacky and supple, but not sticky, until the dough is smooth and elastic, about 8 minutes. If the dough climbs up on the hook, pull it down.

2. **To make the dough by hand,** in a large bowl, combine the water, oil, salt, and yeast. Using a sturdy wooden spoon, stir in enough of the flour to make dough that cannot be stirred. Turn out onto a well-floured work surface. Knead the dough, adding just enough flour as necessary to keep the dough from sticking to the work surface, until the dough is smooth and elastic but slightly tacky to the touch, about 8 minutes.

3. Lightly oil the inside of a medium bowl. Shape the dough into a ball. Place in the bowl and roll the dough to coat with oil. Turn smooth side up and cover tightly with plastic wrap.

4. Let stand in a warm, draft-free place until the dough has doubled in volume (when you insert a finger into the dough, the hole will remain for a few seconds before filling), about 2 hours.

5. **To make the dough ahead,** place the bowl with the dough in the refrigerator. Refrigerate for at least 12 and up to 24 hours to rise slowly. Remove the dough from the refrigerator 1 hour to lose its chill before using.

TIP In this quantity, the quick-rising feature of instant yeast will not be evident. Don't increase the amount of yeast, or the crust will be fluffy and not crisp.

PIZZA RUSTICA

 ith eggplant, Italian sausage, and red peppers, as well as tomato sauce and mozzarella, this pizza has the flavors of the Old Country in every bite. Remember not to layer the ingredients on too heavily, or you will have the pizza maker's nightmare—soggy pizza.

Extra-virgin olive oil

3 slices eggplant, cut into ¼-inch rounds

1 hot or sweet Italian sausage link, casings removed

Pizza Dough (page 96)

Semolina, cornmeal, or whole wheat flour for the pizza peel

½ cup Marinara Sauce (page 141), puréed in a blender or food processor

3 tablespoons freshly grated Parmesan cheese

½ cup (2 ounces) shredded part-skim mozzarella

¼ cup (¼-inch) diced green and/or red bell pepper

Freshly ground black pepper

1. Position a rack in the bottom third of the oven. Place a baking stone on the rack and preheat the oven to 550°F, allowing at least 30 minutes to reach this temperature.

2. Meanwhile, heat ¼ cup of olive oil in a medium skillet over medium-high heat until the oil shimmers. Add the eggplant and cook, turning after 3 minutes, until golden brown and tender, about 6 minutes. Transfer to paper towels to drain and cool.

3. Pour off all but a film of oil from the skillet. Add the sausage and cook over medium heat, breaking up the sausage with the side of a wooden spoon, until it loses its pink color, about 6 minutes. Transfer to the paper towels to drain and cool.

4. Evenly sprinkle a pizza peel with semolina. Following the directions on page 94, shape the dough into a 12-inch round. Transfer to the pizza peel. Brush the dough with olive oil. Spread the sauce over the pizza, leaving a ½-inch border around the perimeter. Sprinkle with the Parmesan, followed by the mozzarella. Coarsely chop the eggplant into bite-sized pieces. Arrange the eggplant, sausage, and bell peppers evenly over the pizza. Season with the pepper.

5. Slide the pizza off the peel onto the stone. Close the door immediately and bake until the crust and the underside is browned (use the peel to lift the pizza and check), 8 to 10 minutes. Use the peel to remove the pizza from the oven and transfer to a carving board. Let stand for 3 minutes. Using a pizza wheel, cut into wedges. Serve immediately.

PIZZA MARGHERITA

MAKES ONE 12-INCH PIZZA, 2 TO 4 SERVINGS

 nly twenty years or so years ago, because fresh mozzarella or basil weren't common in the U.S., one had to travel to Italy to savor this dish. Now we serve hundreds every week at Carrabba's, and that, our friends, is progress. It proves that you don't have to open a can of pizza sauce to make an outstanding pizza.

Pizza Dough (page 96)

Semolina, cornmeal, or whole wheat flour for the pizza peel

Extra-virgin olive oil for brushing

5 ounces fresh whole milk mozzarella, thinly sliced and cut into 2-inch pieces

1½ ripe plum (Roma) tomatoes, cut lengthwise into ¼-inch slices

8 to 10 fresh basil leaves, torn or coarsely chopped

Freshly ground black pepper (optional)

1. Position a rack in the bottom third of the oven. Place a baking stone on the rack and preheat the oven to 550°F, allowing at least 30 minutes to reach this temperature. Evenly sprinkle a pizza peel with semolina.

2. Following the directions on page 94, shape the dough into a 12-inch round. Transfer to the pizza peel. Brush the dough with olive oil. Arrange the mozzarella and tomatoes evenly over the dough, leaving a 1-inch border around the perimeter.

3. Slide the pizza off the peel onto the stone. Close the door immediately and bake until the crust and the underside is browned (use the peel to lift the pizza and check), 8 to 10 minutes. Use the peel to remove the pizza from the oven and transfer to a carving board. Sprinkle with the basil. Let stand for 3 minutes. Season with the pepper, if desired. Using a pizza wheel, cut the dough into wedges and serve hot.

MANGIAMELLI PIZZA

MAKES ONE 12-INCH PIZZA, 2 TO 4 SERVINGS

he Mangiamelli clan is another branch of the family commemorated with a menu item. This one has a little bit of everything . . . kind of like our family!

1 red bell pepper

Pizza Dough (page 96)

Semolina, cornmeal, or whole wheat flour for the pizza peel

Extra-virgin olive oil for brushing

⅔ cup Marinara Sauce (page 141), puréed in a blender or food processor

3 tablespoons freshly grated Parmesan cheese

½ cup (2 ounces) shredded part-skim mozzarella

2 slices dry or Genoa salami, cut into ¼-inch strips

¼ small red onion, thinly sliced

Freshly ground black pepper

1. Position a broiler rack about 8 inches from the source of heat and preheat the broiler on high. Place the bell pepper on the rack and broil, turning occasionally, until the skin is blackened and blistered, about 12 minutes. (You can also cook the pepper on an outdoor grill with direct cooking over high heat.) Transfer to a bowl and let cool. Peel off and discard the blackened skin, and discard the seeds. Cut half of the pepper into 2-by-½-inch strips. Reserve the remaining pepper for another use.

2. Position a rack in the bottom third of the oven. Place a baking stone on the rack and preheat the oven to 550°F, allowing at least 30 minutes to reach this temperature. Evenly sprinkle a pizza peel with semolina.

3. Following the directions on page 94, shape the dough into a 12-inch round. Transfer to the pizza peel. Brush the dough with olive oil. Spread the sauce over the pizza, leaving a ½-inch border around the perimeter. Sprinkle with the Parmesan, followed by the mozzarella. Arrange the salami, red onion, and roasted bell pepper over the pizza. Season with the pepper.

4. Slide the pizza off the peel onto the stone. Close the door immediately and bake until the crust and the underside is browned (use the peel to lift the pizza and check), 8 to 10 minutes. Use the peel to remove the pizza from the oven and transfer to a carving board. Let stand for 3 minutes. Season with the pepper. Using a pizza wheel, cut into wedges. Serve immediately.

PIZZA AL QUATTRO FORMAGGI

MAKES ONE 12-INCH PIZZA, 2 TO 4 SERVINGS

his is sometimes called *Pizza Bianca* *("white pizza")* because it doesn't have the ever-popular tomato sauce. We add a little sun-dried tomato to mix things up a bit. We don't have to tell you to use more of your favorite cheese or to skip what you don't like.

Pizza Dough (page 96)

Semolina, cornmeal, or whole wheat flour for the pizza peel

Extra-virgin olive oil for brushing

¼ cup freshly grated Parmesan cheese

½ cup (2 ounces) shredded fontina cheese

1 ounce rindless goat cheese, crumbled

4 sun-dried tomatoes in oil, drained, cut into ¼-inch strips

3 ounces fresh whole milk mozzarella, thinly sliced and cut into 2-inch pieces

Freshly ground black pepper

1. Position a rack in the bottom third of the oven. Place a baking stone on the rack and preheat the oven to 550°F, allowing at least 30 minutes to reach this temperature. Evenly sprinkle a pizza peel with semolina.

2. Following the directions on page 94, shape the dough into a 12-inch round. Transfer to the pizza peel. Brush the dough with olive oil. Sprinkle with the Parmesan, followed by the fontina and goat cheese, leaving a 1-inch border around the perimeter. Sprinkle with the sun-dried tomatoes. Arrange the mozzarella evenly on top. Season with the pepper.

3. Slide the pizza off the peel onto the stone. Close the door immediately and bake until the crust and the underside is browned (use the peel to lift the pizza and check), 8 to 10 minutes. Use the peel to remove the pizza from the oven and transfer to a carving board. Let stand for 3 minutes. Season with the pepper. Using a pizza wheel, cut the dough into wedges and serve hot.

TIP Sprinkle a couple of tablespoons of chopped fresh basil or oregano on top before serving, if you wish.

PROSCIUTTO AND ARUGULA PIZZA

MAKES ONE 12-INCH PIZZA, 2 TO 4 SERVINGS

oy, talk about not your mama's pizza . . . This fresh-tasting, gorgeous pizza is definitely of the new school, and yet every bit as tasty as the tomato version that has been passed down for generations. The base pizza can be topped with any of your favorite fresh ingredients (baby greens and cherry tomatoes, perhaps) for a personalized variation.

Pizza Dough (page 96)

Semolina, cornmeal, or whole wheat flour for the pizza peel

Extra-virgin olive oil for brushing

3 tablespoons freshly grated Parmesan cheese

1 cup (4 ounces) shredded part-skim mozzarella

Freshly ground black pepper

1 cup baby arugula

2 thin slices prosciutto, each cut into thirds

1 wedge of Parmesan cheese for making shavings

1. Position a rack in the bottom third of the oven. Place a baking stone on the rack and preheat the oven to 550°F, allowing at least 30 minutes to reach this temperature. Evenly sprinkle a pizza peel with semolina.

2. Following the directions on page 94, shape the dough into a 12-inch round. Transfer to the pizza peel. Brush the dough with olive oil. Sprinkle with the Parmesan, followed by the mozzarella, leaving a 1-inch border around the perimeter. Season with the pepper.

3. Slide the pizza off the peel onto the stone. Close the door immediately and bake until the crust and the underside is browned (use the peel to lift the pizza and check), 8 to 10 minutes. Use the peel to remove the pizza from the oven and transfer to a carving board. Let stand for 3 minutes.

4. Using a pizza wheel, cut the dough into 6 wedges. Top each wedge with equal amounts of the arugula and a piece of prosciutto, folded into soft pleats. Using a vegetable peeler, shave Parmesan curls on top. Serve immediately.

TIP If you want to tone down the peppery flavor of the arugula, use mixed baby greens instead.

A dairy food made by separating the liquid whey from milk curds (although ricotta is made from the whey itself), countless varieties of cheese exist. Italian cheeses are renowned for their flavor and quality. We have sourced excellent American-made versions of these classic cheeses, painstakingly made with Old World traditions.

The majority of our cheeses are made by BelGioioso, a Wisconsin company founded by Italian-born Errico Auricchio over thirty years ago. Their award-winning, all-natural cheeses are made with local milk in five separate factories, each one dedicated to a particular kind of cheese, created from traditional recipes.

Cheeses are broadly categorized by their textures: hard or soft. *Hard cheese* is usually grated into fine shreds before use. It can be mixed into food as flavoring, but it is most often grated over the food just before serving as a topping. In Italy, the preferred grating cheese is determined by a general North-South axis, with Romano as the favored grating cheese of the south and Parmesan reigning only in the north.

At Carrabba's, we freshly grate cheese over each serving, just like an Italian home cook. Pre-grated cheese contains preservatives and anti-caking ingredients that just aren't necessary. To grate hard cheese, use the small holes on a box shredder or grate it on a microplane grater. While the latter tool is easiest, it makes very fine, fluffy particles, so you may need more cheese if you are measuring instead of using to taste. (Two ounces of hard cheese makes about ½ cup when grated on a box shredder, but ⅔ cup when prepared with a microplane.) Tightly wrapped in plastic wrap, a chunk of hard cheese keeps in the refrigerator for a month or two.

Here are the grating cheeses we use at Carrabba's:

PARMESAN A grating cheese made from cow's milk with a flavor that is often characterized as nutty. If the cheese is from the Parma region of Italy, it is called Parmigiano-Reggiano or just Parmigiano. It is light yellow, with a hard rind. Don't throw away the rind after grating the softer part. It can be simmered in soup as a flavor booster (remove and discard the rind before eating the soup, though). The domestic Parmesan we use is aged for over 12 months to give it a deliciously mellow, not too sharp, flavor.

RICOTTA SALATA A semi-hard cheese made from salted and pressed ricotta, can be shredded, and its mild flavor is a nice departure from the sharpness of Parmesan.

ROMANO This cheese is all about its piquancy and salty flavor, which can stand up to (and complement) the boldest tomato sauce. It is white and brittle, with a very thin rind. The original version hails from the area around Rome, hence its name. The domestic Romano we use is aged for a year so it is full of flavor.

Soft cheeses are aged for relatively short periods of time, and depending on their moisture content, can be crumbled or shredded on the large holes of a grater. Store them in the refrigerator, tightly wrapped in plastic wrap, for a week or two.

FONTINA Creamy, almost buttery, with a strong earthy note, this cow's milk cheese melts beautifully and smoothly in sauces. Italian fontina d' Aosta is made in the Alps. American fontina is excellent, and may become your favorite for a grilled cheese sandwich.

GOAT CHEESE Tangy goat cheese is often called by its French name (*chèvre*) or, less often, by its Italian (*caprini*). For cooking, buy a rindless goat cheese without any flavorings like garlic or herbs.

GORGONZOLA While this deliciously sharp cow's milk cheese is considered a blue cheese, the mold that provides its distinctive sharpness has a green tint. Domestic gorgonzola comes in two textures, creamy and crumbly. (Italian gorgonzola may be labeled *dolce* or *montagna*.) The latter can be added to salads, and will also melt when stirred into hot sauces, so it is a good all-purpose choice.

MASCARPONE This rich, spreadable cheese is only a step away from thickened cream. We use a luscious domestic version. Sold in 8-ounce or 1-pound tubs in the refrigerated cheese section of most supermarkets, the exact weight may be slightly different if the mascarpone is imported, as those tubs reflect metric weights. Don't worry about the 1-ounce discrepancy, as the small difference won't affect the recipe.

MOZZARELLA Thanks to mozzarella's high moisture content, it is probably the all-time favorite melting cheese. Balls of *fresh milk mozzarella* can be stored in brine or vacuum-packed, and should be used soon (no more than a week) after opening. Fresh mozzarella is too soft to shred, and is sliced by hand. Ours is especially made for us with reduced moisture and sodium content for the best melting texture and flavor. *Low-moisture mozzarella* has had some of the moisture removed, so its shelf life is longer (about a month), and it can be shredded. This is the familiar "pizza" cheese, although we love fresh mozzarella on our pizzas, too, especially the Margherita. Some mozzarella is made from water buffalo milk; we like cow's milk mozzarella. Polly-O, started over a hundred years ago by Italian Giuseppe Pollio, makes most of our top-notch mozzarella and ricotta.

RICOTTA A very soft, spoonable cheese made by coagulating the whey (*ricotta* means "recooked") from making mozzarella. This fresh cheese is an essential ingredient in classic lasagne and Italian-style cheesecake and other dishes. The whole milk or part-skim versions are interchangeable, with the former slightly richer than the latter. (With the additional ingredients added to the cheese, the difference is usually difficult to discern.) Once opened, ricotta only lasts a few days, so plan to use it up. Because it is so wet, ricotta is sometimes drained to remove excess whey before using, as too much moisture could throw off a recipe. To drain one pound of ricotta, line a wire sieve with moistened paper towels, and suspend it over a deep bowl. Add the ricotta and let stand for an hour or so to drain off about ¼ cup of the watery whey.

8

SIDE DISHES

ASPARAGI ALLA ROMANA

 sparagus doesn't need much help to give it a boost of flavor. It is the butter that adds the special touch here (we love olive oil, but it doesn't work the same magic in this dish), along with sharp Romano cheese.

1 pound asparagus, woody stems snapped off

2 tablepoons unsalted butter

Kosher salt and freshly ground black pepper

2 tablespoons freshly grated Romano cheese

1. Bring a large pot of water to a boil over high heat. Add salt to taste. Add the asparagus and cook until barely tender, about 5 minutes. Drain in a colander and rinse under cold running water to stop the cooking. Drain again.

2. Melt the butter in a large saucepan over medium heat. Add the asparagus and cook, turning the asparagus in the butter, until coated and heated through, about 2 minutes. Season with salt and pepper. Transfer to a serving dish. Sprinkle with the Romano cheese and serve hot.

SAUTÉED BROCCOLI WITH RED PEPPERS AND GARLIC

MAKES 6 SERVINGS

here is no need to serve plain broccoli when you can toss this together in a few extra minutes. Don't worry about leftovers. Just heat them up and toss them with some pasta, a little of the pasta cooking water, and Parmesan for an easy lunch.

1 head broccoli, cut into florets, stems peeled and cut into ½-inch-thick slices

1 tablespoon extra-virgin olive oil

½ small red bell pepper, cored and cut into 2-by-¼-inch strips

1 garlic clove, minced

Kosher salt and freshly ground black pepper

1. Bring a large pot of water to a boil over high heat. Add salt to taste. Add the broccoli and cook until crisp-tender, about 4 minutes. Drain in a colander and rinse under cold water to stop the cooking. Drain again.

2. Heat the oil in a large skillet over medium-high heat. Add the red pepper and cook, stirring often, until crisp-tender, about 2 minutes. Stir in the garlic and cook just until fragrant, about 15 seconds. Add the broccoli and cook, stirring occasionally, just until heated through, about 2 minutes. Season with salt and pepper. Transfer to a serving dish and serve hot.

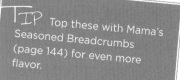
TIP Top these with Mama's Seasoned Breadcrumbs (page 144) for even more flavor.

GARLIC MASHED POTATOES

MAKES 4 SERVINGS

 hese creamy potatoes are one of our most popular side dishes, and for good reason. They are comfort food personified, with loads of personality. They are easier to make than standard mashed potatoes because you don't have to peel the potatoes, and it takes very little effort to roast the garlic.

ROASTED GARLIC

2 large, plump heads of garlic

½ teaspoon extra-virgin olive oil

Kosher salt and freshly ground black pepper

2 pounds red-skinned potatoes, scrubbed but unpeeled, cut into ¾-inch dice

8 tablespoons (1 stick) unsalted butter, at room temperature

½ cup heavy cream, at room temperature

1. To make the roasted garlic, preheat the oven to 325°F. Cut the top ½ inch from each garlic head to reveal the cloves. Discard the tops (or save for another use). Drizzle the cut surfaces with the oil and season with a pinch each of salt and pepper. Place the garlic heads, cut side up, in a small baking dish. Cover the dish tightly with aluminum foil. Bake until the garlic is deep beige and very tender when squeezed, about 1½ hours. Let cool until easy to handle.

2. Put the potatoes in a large saucepan and add enough water to cover. Bring to a boil over high heat. Add salt to taste. Reduce the heat to medium-low and simmer until the potatoes are tender, about 20 minutes. Drain well.

3. Return the potatoes to their cooking pot. Squeeze the garlic from the hulls into a small bowl. Mash with a fork. Add the butter, cream, and roasted garlic. Mash with your favorite method (a masher, a ricer, or an electric mixer) until the potatoes are as smooth as you prefer. Season with salt and pepper. Transfer to a serving bowl and serve hot.

GREEN BEANS WITH ROMANO CRUMBS

MAKES 4 TO 6 SERVINGS

 n the Carrabba and Mandola families, Damian's grandmother, Nonna Testa, reserved this special dish for Sunday meals to serve with the roast. (Try it with the Parsley-Pork Pot Roast on page 35.) Actually, it isn't hard to make at all, and with the tasty, crunchy topping, it is a great way to get kids to eat their vegetables.

1 pound green beans, trimmed and cut into 2-inch lengths

2 tablespoons extra-virgin olive oil

½ cup Mama's Seasoned Breadcrumbs (page 144) or use Italian-style dried breadcrumbs

¼ cup freshly grated Romano cheese

Kosher salt and freshly ground black pepper

1. Preheat the oven to 400°F.

2. Bring a large pot of water to a boil over high heat. Add salt to taste. Add the green beans and cook just until crisp-tender and bright green, about 3 minutes. Drain in a colander and rinse under cold running water to stop the cooking. Drain well and pat dry with paper towels.

3. Toss the green beans and oil in a large bowl. Add the breadcrumbs and Romano cheese and toss again. Season lightly with salt and pepper. Spread in a 2-quart shallow baking dish. (Nonna Testa would take the time to arrange the beans so they all ran in the same direction.)

4. Bake until the crumbs are golden brown, about 20 minutes. Serve hot.

TIP Serve the green beans out of their baking dish, or transfer to a serving bowl.

MASHED POTATOES WITH MASCARPONE

MAKES 4 TO 6 SERVINGS

 es, we know we have another mashed potato recipe in this chapter, but in our book (literally) there is no such thing as too many mashed potatoes! With the rich and creamy mascarpone, you may find yourself pushing the meat aside. These are especially good when serving a roast main course that is on the plain side or one with a lot of gravy.

2 pounds baking potatoes, such as russet or Burbank, peeled and cut into 2-inch chunks

½ cup mascarpone cheese, at room temperature

4 tablespoons (½ stick) unsalted butter, at room temperature

Kosher salt and freshly ground black pepper

1. Put the potatoes in a large saucepan and add enough water to cover. Bring to a boil over high heat. Add salt to taste. Reduce the heat to medium-low and simmer until the potatoes are tender, about 25 minutes. Drain well.

2. Return the potatoes to their cooking pot. Add the mascarpone and butter. Mash with your favorite method (a masher, a ricer, or an electric mixer) until the potatoes are as smooth as you prefer. Season with salt and pepper. Transfer to a serving bowl and serve hot.

ROSEMARY ROASTED POTATOES

MAKES 6 TO 8 SERVINGS

*T*hese potatoes, crispy on the outside and tender within, are a versatile side dish, but they really shine when served with roasts and gravy. Use golden potatoes (Yukon Golds or any of their cousins), which have the right amount of moisture. Baking potatoes are too dry, and red-skinned potatoes are too waxy.

3 pounds Yukon Gold or Yukon Finn potatoes, scrubbed but unpeeled, cut lengthwise into 6 wedges each

1 large yellow onion, cut into ¼-inch-thick half-moons

2 tablespoons extra-virgin olive oil

2 tablespoons coarsely chopped fresh rosemary

Kosher salt and freshly ground black pepper

1. Preheat the oven to 450°F. Place an 18-by-13-inch rimmed baking sheet pan in the oven and heat for 10 minutes.

2. Toss the potato wedges, onion, oil, and rosemary in a large bowl. Remove the baking sheet from the oven. Spread the potato mixture in the hot baking sheet, with the onions underneath the potatoes as much as possible.

3. Return the pan with the potato mixture to the oven and bake for 20 minutes. Turn the potatoes over and continue baking until they are golden brown and tender, 20 to 30 minutes more. Some of the onions may be scorched—if you don't like them that way, remove them. Season with salt and pepper. Transfer to serving bowl and serve hot.

TIP Heat the roasting pan well in the oven so the potatoes will start to cook and brown as soon as they hit the hot metal.

PARMESAN RISOTTO

 his is a basic risotto that we serve as a side dish. To give the risotto its signature creamy texture, be sure to use medium-grain rice for risotto, as it contains a high proportion of starch. Arborio is the easiest to find, but Vialone Nano and Carnaroli are also excellent.

5 cups reduced-sodium chicken broth

2 tablespoons unsalted butter

1 small yellow onion, finely chopped

1⅔ cups (8 ounces) Arborio rice

½ cup (2 ounces) freshly grated Parmesan cheese

Kosher salt and freshly ground black pepper

1. Bring the broth to a simmer in a medium saucepan over high heat. Reduce the heat to very low and keep warm on the stove.

2. Melt the butter in a heavy-bottomed large saucepan or Dutch oven over medium heat. Add the onion and cook, stirring occasionally, until the onion is translucent but not browned, about 3 minutes.

3. Add the rice and stir well until the rice is coated with butter and feels heavy in the spoon, about 2 minutes. Ladle in about ¾ cup of the hot broth. Stir constantly, adjusting the heat as necessary so the rice cooks at a steady simmer without boiling, until almost all of the broth as been absorbed, about 2 minutes. Repeat, stirring in another ¾ cup of broth. Continue, adding broth and stirring almost constantly, until the rice is barely tender, about 20 minutes. If you run out of broth before the rice is tender, use hot water. Stir in the Parmesan. Season with salt and pepper. Add enough broth or hot water to give the risotto a loose, but not soupy, consistency. Serve hot.

NOTE *The risotto can be made up to 2 hours ahead, kept at room temperature. Cook it just until al dente, about 15 minutes. Spread on an oiled rimmed baking sheet and cover with plastic wrap. When ready to serve, reheat the stock. Melt an additional 1 tablespoon of butter in the saucepan. Add the risotto, and continue the cooking process, adding warm stock and stirring, until the rice is barely tender and hot, about 5 minutes.*

ZUCCHINI STEFANO

ccasionally we name a dish for someone who we are not related to. Steven Shlemon, Carrabba's president, is certainly family. We serve this sautéed zucchini with quick tomato sauce as a side dish, but tossed with pasta, it could become dinner.

3 tablespoons finely chopped yellow onion

2 tablespoons extra-virgin olive oil

4 medium zucchini, trimmed and cut into ¼-inch rounds

½ teaspoon Grill Seasoning (page 146)

1 cup Picchi Pacchiu Sauce (page 90)

2 tablespoons freshly grated Parmesan cheese for serving

1. Heat the onion and oil together in a large skillet over medium heat, stirring occasionally, until the onion is softened, about 3 minutes.

2. Add the zucchini and season with the grill seasoning. Cook, stirring occasionally, until the zucchini is crisp-tender, about 3 minutes more.

3. Stir in the picchi pacchiu sauce and bring to a simmer, stirring often. Transfer to a serving dish, sprinkle with the Parmesan cheese, and serve hot.

TIP Substitute blanched green beans (see page 112) for the zucchini, but only cook with the onion until heated through, about 2 minutes, before adding the sauce.

SIDE DISHES

117

NONNA'S SAVORY SQUASH CASSEROLE

MAKES 4 TO 6 SERVINGS

During the summer, bright yellow squash is abundant. It's pretty, but it isn't the tastiest vegetable on the block and Southern cooks have long turned it into a casserole to dress it up. Nonna added some Italian touches to make it her own. Serve it with just about anything.

¼ cup extra-virgin olive oil

1 yellow onion, chopped

1 celery rib, thinly sliced

2 garlic cloves, minced

2 pounds yellow squash, trimmed, cut into ¼-inch rounds

Softened butter, for the pie dish

1 cup Mama's Seasoned Breadcrumbs (page 144) or Italian-seasoned breadcrumbs

¼ cup (1 ounce) freshly grated Romano cheese

2 large eggs, beaten

2 scallions, white and green parts, thinly sliced

2 tablespoons chopped fresh flat-leaf parsley

1 teaspoon kosher salt

½ teaspoon freshly ground black pepper

½ cup Homemade Plain Breadcrumbs (page 144) or use dried plain breadcrumbs

2 tablespoons unsalted butter, cut into small cubes

1. Heat the oil in a very large skillet over medium heat. Add the onion and cook, stirring occasionally, until golden and the edges are beginning to brown, about 5 minutes. Stir in the celery and garlic. Add the squash and cook, stirring occasionally, until the squash is very tender and the juices have evaporated, about 15 minutes. Transfer to a large bowl and let cool until tepid.

2. Preheat the oven to 400°F. Lightly butter a 9-inch glass pie pan or 1-quart gratin dish.

3. Add Mama's Seasoned Breadcrumbs, Romano, eggs, scallions, parsley, salt, and pepper to the squash mixture and mix well. Spread in the pie plate. Top with the Homemade Plain Breadcrumbs and dot with the butter cubes.

4. Bake until bubbling and the top is golden brown, about 20 minutes. Let cool slightly, and serve.

9

DESSERTS

RASPBERRY TARTLETS

Looking for a fruit dessert that's not too sweet, but is still the perfect finish to the meal? Try these beautiful fruit tartlets that look like they came right out of the bakery. While there is something special about serving individual tarts to guests, we've also provided a variation for a single large tart. Tartlet pans can be found at specialty kitchenware shops and online.

PASTRY DOUGH

1½ cups all-purpose flour

1 teaspoon granulated sugar

¼ teaspoon salt

8 tablespoons (1 stick) cold unsalted butter, cut into ½-inch cubes

2 large egg yolks

2 tablespoons ice-cold water

6 tablespoons raspberry preserves

1½ packages (9 ounces total) fresh raspberries

Confectioners' sugar for serving

Whipped cream or vanilla ice cream for serving

1. To make the dough, mix the flour, sugar, and salt together in a large bowl. Add the butter cubes and toss to coat them with flour. Using a pastry blender or 2 knives, cut the butter into the flour until the mixture looks like coarse meal with some pea-sized pieces of butter. Mix the eggs and water together. Gradually stir in the yolk mixture, stirring until the mixture is thoroughly moistened and begins to clump. (The mixture may look crumbly, but if you press it together, it will hold together. If not, add water, a teaspoon at a time.) Gather up into a thick disk and wrap in plastic wrap. Refrigerate until chilled, 1 to 2 hours.

2. Lightly butter six 4-by-¾-inch tartlet pans with removable bottoms. Cut the dough into 6 equal pieces, and shape each piece into a 3-inch diameter disk. One at a time, place a disk on a lightly floured work surface, and dust the top with flour. Roll out into a ⅛-inch thick round. Fit into a tartlet pan. Using the heel of your hand, press the overhanging dough around the rim of the pan to remove the excess dough. Pierce the dough a few times with a fork. Refrigerate the tartlets for 15 to 30 minutes.

TIPS Another time, substitute fresh blueberries and blueberry preserves for the raspberries and raspberry preserves.

To save time, bake the shells a day ahead and store in an airtight container. It will only take a few minutes to fill them.

3. Preheat the oven to 400°F. Line each tartlet with a round of parchment paper or aluminum foil. Fill with aluminum pie weights or dry beans. Place on a large baking sheet. Bake until the edges of the pastry look set and are beginning to brown, about 12 minutes. Remove from the oven and remove the weights in their paper. Return to the oven and bake until the tart shells are crisp and lightly browned, about 6 minutes more. Transfer the pans to a wire cake rack and let cool.

4. Spread 1 tablespoon preserves in each pastry shell. Arrange about 11 raspberries, rounded ends up, in each shell. Just before serving, remove the sides of the pans and place a tartlet on a plate. Sift confectioners' sugar over each tartlet and serve with a dollop of whipped cream. (The tartlets can be made up to 1 day ahead, loosely covered with plastic wrap and refrigerated.)

LARGE RASPBERRY TART *Roll out the entire disk of dough into a 13-inch round about* ⅛*-inch thick. Fit into a 9-inch diameter tart pan with a removable bottom. Pierce with a fork. Refrigerate for 30 minutes. Line with parchment paper and pastry weights and bake until the pastry looks set, 12 to 15 minutes. Remove parchment and weights and continue baking until golden brown, about 10 minutes more. Cool completely. Fill with ½ cup raspberry preserves, and top with 2½ boxes (15 ounces) fresh raspberries.*

LEMON ROSEMARY POUND CAKE

his simple quick bread is a good example of Italian-American cooking, taking Old World flavors and giving them a lift. The fresh-from-the-oven cake smells so delicious that you will find it hard to wait until it cools completely, so we just eat it warm!

CAKE

1½ cups unbleached all-purpose flour, plus more for the pan

¼ teaspoon baking powder

¼ teaspoon baking soda

¼ teaspoon salt

8 tablespoons (1 stick) unsalted butter, at room temperature, plus more for the pan

1 cup sugar

Grated zests of 2 lemons (save the lemons for the syrup)

2 large eggs, beaten

½ teaspoon vanilla extract

½ cup buttermilk

2 teaspoons finely chopped fresh rosemary

SYRUP

½ cup fresh lemon juice (from about 3 large lemons)

½ cup sugar

Two 3-inch sprigs fresh rosemary

1. To make the cake, preheat the oven to 350°F. Lightly butter an 8½-by-4½-inch loaf pan. Line the bottom with waxed paper. Dust the pan with flour and tap out the excess.

2. Sift the flour, baking powder, baking soda, and salt together. Beat the butter, sugar, and lemon zest together in a medium bowl with an electric mixer set on high speed until the mixture is light in color and texture, about 3 minutes. Gradually beat in the eggs, then the vanilla, scraping down the sides of the bowl as needed. Reduce the mixer speed to low. In thirds, alternating with two equal additions of buttermilk, add the flour mixture, scraping down the sides of the bowl as needed. Mix in the chopped rosemary. Beat just until smooth. Spread in the pan and smooth the top.

3. Bake until the top of the cake is golden brown and a wooden toothpick inserted in the center comes out clean, about 1 hour. Transfer the pan to a wire cake rack and let cool for 10 to 15 minutes.

4. Meanwhile, make the syrup. Bring the lemon juice, sugar, and rosemary sprigs to a boil in a nonreactive small saucepan over medium-high heat, stirring to dissolve the sugar. Let boil without stirring until reduced by half, about 7 minutes. Remove the rosemary sprigs. Let cool slightly.

5. Pierce the cake about a dozen times with a long bamboo skewer or toothpick. Gradually pour the syrup evenly over the cake. Let cool for 30 minutes. (Or let the cake cool completely.)

6. Invert the cake onto a serving platter and remove the waxed paper. Cut into slices and serve warm.

LIMONCELLO BREAD PUDDING

MAKES 6 SERVINGS

imoncello is a lemon-based liqueur, and many households in Sicily make a homemade version from the lemons growing in their backyards. Traditionally served ice cold after dinner, it is also a fantastic ingredient in desserts, as shown in this citrus-flavored bread pudding. It's a huge favorite at Carrabba's—comfort food, Italian-style.

BREAD PUDDING

Softened butter for the baking dish

5 large eggs

⅔ cup sugar

⅓ cup limoncello

1 teaspoon vanilla extract

1¼ cups whole milk

1¼ cups heavy cream

6 cups (1-inch) cubed egg bread, such as brioche or challah (about 12 ounces)

LIMONCELLO SYRUP

½ cup limoncello

½ cup sugar

Vanilla ice cream for serving

6 fresh mint sprigs for garnish

1. Preheat the oven to 325°F. Lightly butter an 11½-by-8-inch baking dish.

2. Whisk the eggs, sugar, limoncello, and vanilla together in a large bowl. Gradually whisk in the milk and cream. Add the bread cubes and stir. Let stand until the bread has absorbed some of the liquid, about 15 minutes. Pour into the baking dish.

3. Bake until gently puffed and a knife inserted in the center comes out clean, about 45 minutes. To serve warm, let cool for 5 minutes. Or cool, cover with plastic wrap, and refrigerate for up to 2 days, and serve chilled.

4. Meanwhile, make the limoncello syrup. Bring the limoncello and sugar to a boil in a small saucepan over high heat, stirring constantly until the sugar is completely dissolved. Let boil without stirring for 1 minute to reduce slightly. Remove from the heat. Use the syrup while it is warm.

5. Cut the warm pudding into 6 equal pieces. Put each pudding portion in a bowl, top each with a scoop of ice cream, and drizzle with the warm syrup. Garnish each with a mint sprig and serve at once.

TIP If you can't find an egg bread, use firm bread without a lot of air pockets to make the puddings. Sourdough bread doesn't make good bread pudding.

APPLE CROSTADA

MAKES 6 SERVINGS

*A*t Carrabba's, we serve these warm, free-form apple tarts in individual cast-iron skillets, and if you own a set, they do make a very nice presentation. But the crostadas are so delicious that you can serve them on your plainest everyday plates, and they will still disappear.

LARGE BATCH PASTRY DOUGH

2¼ cups all-purpose flour

1 tablespoon sugar

¼ teaspoon salt

12 tablespoons (1½ sticks) cold, unsalted butter, cut into ½-inch cubes

3 large egg yolks

2 tablespoons ice-cold water

NUT SUGAR

¼ cup coarsely chopped walnuts

1 tablespoon sugar

1 tablespoon all-purpose flour

FILLING

3 Granny Smith apples, peeled, cored, and cut into halves

6 teaspoons sugar

2 tablespoons cold, unsalted butter, cut into 6 equal pats

2 tablespoons unsalted butter, melted and cooled to tepid, for brushing

6 tablespoons store-bought caramel sauce for serving

Vanilla ice cream for serving

1. To make the dough, follow the instructions on page 122 and refrigerate for 1 to 2 hours.

2. To make the nut sugar, pulse the walnuts, sugar, and flour together in a food processor until very finely chopped into a powder. Pour into a small bowl and set aside.

3. Preheat racks in the top and center of the oven and preheat to 400°F. Line 2 large baking sheets with parchment paper.

4. Cut the dough into 6 equal pieces, and shape each piece into a 3-inch diameter disk. One at a time, place a disk on a lightly floured work surface, and dust the top with flour. Roll out into a 7-inch-diameter round about ⅛-inch thick. Sprinkle 1 tablespoon of the nut sugar in the center of the round, leaving a 1-inch border. Cut an apple half into 10 to 12 thin wedges. Arrange the wedges, overlapping as needed, in a pinwheel pattern

TIP Italians don't cook with a lot of cinnamon, but if you like it, sprinkle a large pinch over the apples before baking.

over the nut sugar. Sprinkle with 1 teaspoon
of sugar. Bring up the edges of the dough, pleating and folding
as needed, to partly cover the apples, leaving the center exposed. Pinch any cracked dough closed. Cut or break a butter pat into a few pieces and dot over the apples. Slip a metal spatula under the crostada and transfer to the baking sheet.

5. Brush the dough with the melted butter. Bake, switching the sheets from top to bottom halfway through baking, until the crust is golden brown and the apples are just tender, about 30 minutes. Let cool for 10 minutes. Place each crostada in an individual skillet (or on a plate). Top with caramel sauce and a scoop of ice cream. Serve warm.

RICOTTA CHEESECAKE

MAKES 16 SERVINGS

T here's more than one way to make a cheesecake, and for all its popularity in America, the cream cheese–based version could stand some competition. In Sicily, ricotta is the cheese of choice, making a towering masterpiece of a dessert that is light-textured but substantial at the same time. This is not a last-minute dessert, but its memory will linger.

RICH PASTRY DOUGH

2¼ cups all-purpose flour

½ cup sugar

¼ teaspoon salt

14 tablespoons (1¾ sticks) cold, unsalted butter, cut into ½-inch cubes

1 large egg plus 2 large egg yolks

1 teaspoon vanilla extract

Grated zest of ½ orange

Softened butter for the baking pan

CHEESECAKE

⅓ cup spiced or dark rum

¾ cup golden raisins

2 pounds part-skim or whole milk ricotta cheese

1 cup sugar

½ cup Homemade Plain Breadcrumbs (page 144) or dried plain breadcrumbs

6 large eggs, separated, at room temperature

⅓ cup heavy cream

⅓ cup sour cream

1½ teaspoons vanilla extract

Grated zest of 1 orange

¼ teaspoon salt

1. To make the rich pastry dough, pulse the flour, sugar, and salt together in a food processor fitted with the metal blade to combine. Add the butter and pulse about 7 times until the mixture resembles coarse breadcrumbs with some pea-sized pieces. Transfer to a bowl. (Or combine the dry ingredients in a medium bowl, and cut in the butter with a pastry blender.) Mix the egg, yolks, vanilla, and orange zest together in a small bowl. Pour over the dry ingredients and stir the dough clumps together. Gather into a thick disk and wrap in plastic wrap. Refrigerate until chilled, 1 to 2 hours. The dough is easiest to work with when chilled and pliable, but not ice-cold and rock-hard.

2. Lightly butter a 9-by-3-inch springform pan. Generously flour a work surface. Unwrap the dough, place on the work surface, and dust the top with flour. Roll out the dough into a 16-inch round about ⅛-inch thick, being sure the dough doesn't stick to the work surface (slide a long knife under the dough to loosen it, if necessary). Transfer the dough to the pan, lining the bottom and sides with dough. Do not worry if it breaks apart— just piece and press it together. Trim the excess dough flush with the top of the pan. Refrigerate the pan while making the filling.

3. To make the cheesecake, preheat the oven to 350°F. Heat the rum just until warm in a saucepan or microwave oven, add the raisins, and let stand to plump the raisins for 10 minutes. Drain, reserving the rum.

4. Line a colander with moistened paper towels. Add the ricotta and cover with more towels. Place a plate to fit over the ricotta. Press firmly to extract 3 to 4 tablespoons whey from the ricotta.

5. Discarding the whey and paper towels, transfer the ricotta to a large bowl. Add the sugar and mix with an electric mixer set on high speed until combined, about 30 seconds. Add the reserved rum with the breadcrumbs, eggs, heavy cream, sour cream, vanilla, orange zest, and salt and mix just until smooth, about 30 seconds more. Stir in the drained raisins. Pour into the dough-lined pan.

6. Place the pan on a rimmed baking sheet. Bake for 1 hour. Reduce the oven temperature to 325°F and continue baking until the top of the filling is golden brown and the crust is shrinking from the sides of the pan, about 30 minutes more. Let cool in the turned-off oven with the oven door held ajar with a wooden spoon for 1 hour. Transfer the pan to a wire cake rack and let cool completely.

7. Remove the pan sides. Wrap the cheesecake in plastic wrap and refrigerate until chilled, at least 4 hours or overnight. Use a thin-bladed knife dipped in cold water between slices to cut into wedges. Serve chilled or at room temperature.

SOGNO DI CIOCCOLATA

 iterally, "chocolate dream," here's a dessert that chocolate lovers will never forget—brownies layered with chocolate mousse and whipped cream, doused with coffee liqueur. It's another fan favorite that you can now make at home.

BROWNIE LAYER

1½ cups sugar

12 tablespoons (1½ sticks) unsalted butter, melted

1½ teaspoons vanilla extract

3 large eggs, at room temperature

¾ cup all-purpose flour

½ cup Dutch-processed cocoa powder

¼ teaspoon baking powder

¼ teaspoon salt

MOUSSE

1 cup heavy cream

6 ounces semisweet chocolate, coarsely chopped

WHIPPED CREAM

1 cup heavy cream

2 tablespoons confectioners' sugar

½ teaspoon vanilla extract

¼ cup Kahlúa or other coffee liqueur

1 cup store-bought chocolate syrup for serving

1. For the brownie layers, preheat the oven to 350°F. Lightly butter two 8-inch square baking pans. Line the bottoms of the pans with parchment or waxed paper.

2. Whisk the sugar, melted butter, and vanilla together in large bowl. One at a time, whisk in the eggs. Sift the flour, cocoa, baking powder, and salt together. Add to the butter mixture and stir until smooth. Divide the batter evenly among the pans and smooth the tops.

3. Bake until the brownies are beginning to pull away from sides, about 20 minutes. Transfer to wire cake racks and let cool in the pans. Invert and unmold onto the racks and remove the parchment paper.

continues

DESSERTS

133

4. For the mousse, bring the cream to a simmer in a medium saucepan. Remove from the heat. Add the chocolate and let stand until the chocolate softens, about 1 minute. Whisk until smooth. Pour into a medium bowl. Refrigerate until the chocolate mixture is cool and barely beginning to set, about 30 minutes.

5. For the whipped cream, whip the cream, confectioners' sugar, and vanilla in a chilled medium bowl with an electric mixer set on high until the cream is stiff.

6. Place 1 brownie layer in a clean 8-by-8-inch baking pan. Brush with 2 tablespoons of liqueur. Whisk the cooled chocolate mixture just until lightened in color and fluffy. Do not overbeat the mousse or it may separate. Spread half of the chocolate mousse on the brownie in the pan, and spread with a thin layer of the whipped cream. Repeat with the remaining brownie, liqueur, mousse, and whipped cream. Cover and refrigerate until chilled, at least 2 hours. (The dessert can be refrigerated for up to 1 day.) Remove from the refrigerator about 15 minutes before serving.

7. To serve, cut into 9 squares. Place a square in a shallow bowl and drizzle with as much chocolate sauce as you like. Serve chilled.

TIRAMISÙ

here are a zillion recipes for this now-classic Italian dolce. *We'll put ours against any one (or all!) of them for a tiramisù smackdown. (*Tiramisù *means* pick me up *in Italian, but you probably knew that already.) The filling usually contains raw eggs, but our version heats them to kill any potentially harmful bacteria. Even if you think you have a great tiramisù recipe, get ready to toss it out in favor of this beauty.*

2 large eggs

⅓ cup plus 1 tablespoon sugar

1 tablespoon dark rum, such as Myer's

½ teaspoon vanilla extract

1 container (16 to 17 ounces) mascarpone

2 cups brewed Italian roast coffee, cooled

2 tablespoons hazelnut liqueur, such as Frangelico

2 tablespoons coffee liqueur, such as Tia Maria

32 dry ladyfingers *(savoiardi)*, about 9 ounces

1 bar (3½ ounces) semisweet or bittersweet chocolate, grated on the large holes of a box grater

TIP To use soft ladyfingers, let them stand, uncovered, at room temperature overnight to stale before using, as fresh ones will soak up too much espresso.

1. Whisk the eggs, sugar, and rum together in the insert part of a double boiler. Heat over simmering water, being sure that the bottom of the insert does not touch the water, using a rubber spatula to stir constantly and scrape down splashes on the inside of the insert, until the mixture is hot, thickened, and opaque, and reaches 160°F on an instant-read thermometer. Turn off the heat and stir for 1 minute longer.

2. Remove the insert from the pot. Add the vanilla. Beat with an electric mixer set on high speed until the mixture is cooled and tripled in volume, about 3 minutes. (It should look like old-fashioned shaving cream.) A few tablespoons at a time, beat in the mascarpone. Do not overbeat.

3. Have a 9-inch-square baking dish ready to hold the tiramisù. Mix the coffee and liqueurs together in a wide, shallow bowl. One at a time, quickly dip 16 ladyfingers in the coffee mixture (do not soak them), and place side-by-side to line the bottom of the baking dish. Spread with half of the mascarpone mixture, then sprinkle with half of the chocolate. Repeat with the remaining ladyfingers (discard the remaining coffee mixture), mascarpone, and top with the chocolate. Cover with plastic wrap and refrigerate until chilled, at least 4 hours or overnight. Spoon into bowls and serve chilled.

DESSERTS

10

BASICS AND SAUCES

ALFREDO SAUCE

*W*e use this sauce to give a rich creaminess reminiscent of the original sauce for Fettuccine Alfredo, a famous dish that originated at the restaurant of the same name in Rome in the 1920s. (Yes, we know: the original has only butter and Parmesan cheese, but this is inspired by, and not a replica of, the classic.) It is super-easy to make, so prepare it just before using.

4 tablespoons (½ stick) unsalted butter

1 cup heavy cream

1 cup whole milk

Kosher salt and freshly ground black pepper

1. Melt the butter in a small saucepan over medium heat. Add the cream and milk and bring to a simmer, stirring occasionally, being sure that the mixture doesn't boil over. Simmer until slightly reduced, about 2 minutes. Season with salt and pepper. (The sauce can be made up to 2 hours ahead, kept at room temperature.)

BASIL PESTO

MAKES ABOUT 1½ CUPS

esto *(from the Italian* pestare, *to grind) has countless uses in the Italian kitchen beyond mixing with pasta. Stir it into soup to give a nice flavor boost, or spread it on pizza dough as an alternative to tomato sauce. Try it on sandwiches as a condiment. In short: Make some!*

2 garlic cloves

¾ packed fresh basil leaves

¼ cup packed fresh flat-leaf parsley leaves

¼ cup coarsely chopped walnuts

¼ cup freshly grated Romano cheese

¼ cup freshly grated Parmesan cheese

2 tablespoons pine nuts

½ teaspoon kosher salt

¼ teaspoon freshly ground black pepper

½ cup extra-virgin olive oil, plus more for topping the pesto

1. With the machine running, drop the garlic through the feed tube of a food processor fitted with the metal chopping blade to mince the garlic. Add the remaining ingredients, except the olive oil, and pulse a few times until finely chopped.

2. With the machine running, gradually pour in the olive oil. Transfer the pesto to an airtight container and smooth the top. Pour a thin layer of olive oil on the pesto to seal it. (The pesto can be refrigerated for up to 2 weeks. Replace the oil topping as you use the pesto. Or freeze the pesto for up to 5 months, defrosting in the refrigerator overnight before use.)

TIP You can use either walnuts or pine nuts if you don't want to combine them.

LEMON BUTTER SAUCE

MAKES ABOUT 1 CUP

e have many "secret ingredients" at Carrabba's. But it is our lemon butter sauce that gives some of our most popular dishes a wonderful creaminess and mild tang. A variation on the classic beurre blanc ("white butter" in French), there is a trick to its success. Cook it over the very lowest heat so the butter can soften into a beautiful sauce. Once you get the hang of it, you will love making this sauce as much as you'll love eating it.

12 tablespoons (1½ sticks) cold unsalted butter, cut into ½-inch pieces, divided

2 tablespoons finely chopped yellow onion

2 garlic cloves, minced

⅓ cup dry white wine, such as Cavit Pinot Grigio

3 tablespoons fresh lemon juice

Kosher salt and freshly ground white pepper

1. Melt 1 tablespoon of the butter in a nonreactive medium skillet over medium heat. Add the onion and garlic and cook, stirring often, until the onion is translucent but not browned, about 3 minutes. Add the wine and lemon juice and bring to a boil over high heat. Cook until the liquid is reduced to about 2 tablespoons, about 3 minutes.

2. Reduce the heat to its very lowest setting. A few pieces at a time, whisk in the butter, letting the first addition melt before adding more butter. Be sure that the butter is softening into an emulsified sauce, and not melting. With practice, you will be able to increase the heat a bit to speed the softening. It should take you about 3 minutes to add all of the butter and "build" the sauce. Season with salt and pepper. Remove from the heat.

3. The sauce can be stored at room temperature for up to 2 hours. Remember, it will be reheated in each recipe. *Be sure to heat the sauce over very low heat when reheating*, or it will separate. (That is, it will look like melted butter and not an emulsified sauce.) If this happens, remember it will still taste the same!

MARINARA SAUCE

 ariners (that is, fishermen) would make this quick sauce onboard ship as a cooking medium for seafood. It is nicely spiced with red pepper flakes and oregano, and we hope that you try it with the anchovies, which add extra flavor without a fishy taste—we promise.

2 tablespoons extra-virgin olive oil

1 small yellow onion, finely chopped

2 scallions, white and green parts, finely chopped

2 anchovy fillets in oil, drained and finely chopped (optional)

4 garlic cloves, minced

¼ cup hearty red wine, such as Citra Montepulciano

1 can (28 ounces) whole tomatoes in juice

1 teaspoon dried oregano

¼ teaspoon crushed hot red pepper flakes

¼ teaspoon freshly ground black pepper

1. Heat the oil in a medium saucepan over medium heat. Add the onion and cook, stirring occasionally, until translucent, about 5 minutes. Add the scallions, anchovies (if using), and garlic and cook, stirring occasionally, until the garlic is fragrant, about 1 minute.

2. Add the wine. Pour the tomatoes and their juices into a bowl, crush the tomatoes between your fingers, and pour the mixture into the saucepan. Add the oregano, hot pepper flakes, and pepper and bring to a simmer. Reduce the heat to medium-low. Simmer, stirring often, until the tomato juices have thickened and the sauce has reduced slightly, about 30 minutes. (The sauce can be cooled, covered, and refrigerated for up to 3 days. Or freeze for up to 2 months and thaw overnight in the refrigerator before using.)

VARIATION *To make Boscaiola Sauce, a nice tomato sauce with "woodland" mushrooms (bosca means forest in Italian), heat 1 tablespoon extra-virgin olive oil in a medium skillet over medium-high heat. Add 8 ounces white mushrooms, sliced, and cook, stirring often, until lightly browned, about 6 minutes. Stir into the sauce during the last 10 minutes of simmering. It makes a fine topping for polenta, as pictured on page 32.*

THE CARRABBA'S WAY *Tomatoes*

A fresh, juicy tomato is a summertime treat. Unfortunately, the window of opportunity to savor this delight is short. Luckily, when the season is over, canned tomatoes are used to make terrific pasta sauce and other traditional dishes. Where would Carrabba's be without the treasure trove of tomato sauce recipes that we inherited from the Carrabba and Mandola families, and continue to gather during our annual recipe-collecting sojourns to Italy?

Our pasta sauces are made from scratch in each restaurant, and never shipped in from a commissary. We have sourced the very best canned tomatoes in the country, grown under perfect conditions in California's Central Valley. Our vendor has family roots in Tuscany and Liguria, and their tomatoes are grown with respect for the land gained from generations of experience. Their tomatoes are harvested and canned once a year at their summertime ultimate flavorful peak—in fact, only six hours lapse from the time the tomato is picked to when it is the can. We run frequent taste tests to be sure that our high standards are being met. After all, nothing but the best for our kitchens . . . and our guests!

We would tell the name of our purveyor, but they don't sell at the retail level. Here are some general shopping tips:

WHEN PURCHASING CANNED TOMATOES AT THE SUPERMARKET, skip over the flavored varieties. They may be timesavers, but you will have more control over ingredients. (And really, our sauces only use a few well-chosen ingredients, and it doesn't take long to chop an onion and a few garlic cloves.) Buy whole plum or pear-shaped tomatoes in juice, as they have the meatiest texture and richest juice. The tomatoes should be plump and unblemished, and the packing juice thick, bright red, and tasty enough to drink on its own.

CANNED TOMATOES SHOULD BE CHOPPED OR CRUSHED BEFORE USE so they can break down a bit during cooking. You do not have to take out a knife and chop them by hand—what a mess! Simply pour the tomatoes (and their juice, if the recipe calls for it) into a deep bowl. Squeeze the tomatoes through your clean fingers (watch out for squirting juice) until you get the desired texture—the majority of pieces should be about the size of a quarter or smaller. You can buy diced canned tomatoes, but these tomatoes have been chemically treated to retain their cube shape. Even with long cooking, they won't break down. But if you like chunky tomato sauce or tomatoes that hold their shape in soup, then diced tomatoes are an option.

TOMATO SAUCE "POMODORO"

MAKES ABOUT 1 QUART

 e love this sauce, a specialty of Mama Mandola's. Not to cast stones, but some people get their tomato sauce sweet by adding sugar. Mama knew to cook the onions until they are golden brown in order to bring out their sweetness the natural way. Pomodoro means "tomato" in Italian, so we call this "Pomo Sauce" for short in the kitchen to differentiate it from its cousins, Marinara and Amatriciana.

1 yellow onion, finely chopped

¼ cup extra-virgin olive oil

4 garlic cloves, minced

1 can (28 ounces) whole tomatoes in juice

Kosher salt and freshly ground black pepper

¼ cup coarsely chopped fresh basil

1. Combine the onion and oil in a medium saucepan over medium heat. Cook, stirring occasionally, until the onion is golden brown and just beginning to caramelize, about 12 minutes. Add the garlic and stir until fragrant, about 1 minute.

2. Pour the tomatoes and their juices into a bowl. Crush the tomatoes between your fingers. Pour the tomatoes and their juices into the saucepan and bring to a simmer. Reduce the heat to medium-low. Simmer, stirring often, until the tomato juices have thickened and the sauce has reduced slightly, about 20 minutes. Season with salt and pepper.

3. Remove from the heat. Sprinkle the basil over the sauce and cover with the lid. Let stand 5 minutes. Stir in the basil. (The sauce can be cooled, covered, and refrigerated for up to 3 days. Or freeze for up to 2 months and thaw overnight in the refrigerator before using.)

TIP To avoid bruising the basil, Mama tore the leaves into pieces with her fingers. Chopping is fine, but you won't have basil-scented fingers.

MAMA'S SEASONED BREADCRUMBS

MAKES ABOUT 5½ CUPS

*D*on't underestimate this unassuming ingredient. There was a time when every Italian-American kitchen had a jar of seasoned crumbs in the pantry —it was used up so fast, it didn't need to be stored in the freezer as we recommend here. Take a little time and make these—you won't be sorry.

5 cups Homemade Plain Breadcrumbs (below) or dried plain breadcrumbs

½ cup freshly grated Romano cheese

3 scallions, white and green parts, coarsely chopped

3 garlic cloves, coarsely chopped

1 teaspoon kosher salt

1 teaspoon freshly ground black pepper

1. Pulse all of the ingredients in a food processor fitted with the metal chopping blade about 10 times, or until the scallions and garlic are very finely minced. Transfer to an airtight container. (The breadcrumbs can be frozen for up to 1 month. Remove the amount you need from the container, and let thaw at room temperature for 15 minutes before using.)

   VARIATION: *To make Homemade Plain Breadcrumbs, a daily staple in most Italian-American households, preheat the oven to 175°F. Cut 8 ounces of day-old crusty Italian-style bread into 1-inch cubes. Spread the cubes on a large rimmed baking sheet. Bake, stirring occasionally, until the cubes are crisp and the edges are beginning to brown, about 45 minutes. Let cool completely.*

   In batches, process the cubes in a food processor fitted with the metal chopping blade until very fine, about 1½ minutes. Transfer to an airtight container. (The breadcrumbs can be frozen for up to 1 month. Remove the amount you need from the container, and let defrost at room temperature for 15 minutes before using.)
   Makes 5 cups.

TIP Let the bread stand out uncovered at room temperature for a day or two to stale.

GRILL BASTE

 hhhh. Here's another secret ingredient that gives our food its special flavor. Instead of using plain oil for brushing on food before grilling, we use this basting mixture. You can substitute olive oil for the butter if necessary. Or use this and sit back and gather the compliments.

2 tablespoons unsalted butter

1 small yellow onion, finely chopped

4 garlic cloves, chopped

1 tablespoon all-purpose flour

½ cup extra-virgin olive oil

¼ cup red wine vinegar

2 tablespoons fresh lemon juice

1 tablespoon Dijon mustard

1½ tablespoons sugar

2 tablespoons finely chopped fresh flat-leaf parsley

1. Melt the butter in a medium saucepan over medium heat. Add the onion and cook until softened, about 2 minutes. Add the garlic and cook until the onion is translucent, about 2 minutes. Sprinkle in the flour, stir well, and cook without browning for 1 minute. Whisk in the oil, vinegar, lemon juice, mustard, and sugar. Bring to a boil and reduce the heat to medium-low. Add the parsley and cook, whisking often, until lightly thickened, about 5 minutes. Let cool. The baste will separate. Whisk well before using. (The grill baste can be made up to 1 week ahead, cooled, covered, and refrigerated. Bring to room temperature before using.)

GRILL SEASONING

MAKES ABOUT ½ CUP

hy use salt and pepper when you can use this zesty blend of herbs and spices? A sprinkle of this seasoning on meat, chicken, and seafood really makes the food sing. It will keep in a cool, dark cupboard indefinitely, but you will use it up too quickly for it to go stale.

¼ cup kosher salt

2 tablespoons freshly ground black pepper

1½ teaspoons granulated garlic

1½ teaspoons granulated onion

1½ teaspoons dry oregano

¼ teaspoon crushed hot red pepper

1. Mix all of the ingredients together in a small bowl. Transfer to an airtight container. (The seasoning can be stored in a cool, dark place indefinitely.)

TIP Granulated garlic and granulated onion are gritty and not pulverized like their powdered versions. They are easy to find at supermarkets and online.

INDEX

Note: Page references in *italics* indicate photographs.